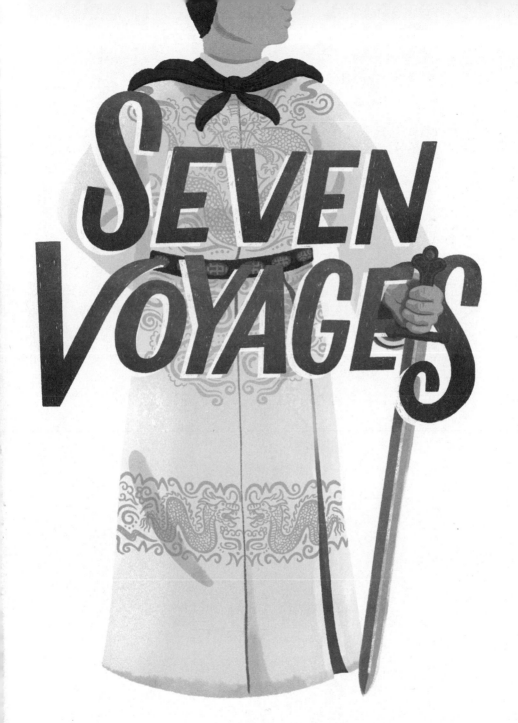

SEVEN VOYAGES

How China's Treasure Fleet Conquered the Sea

Laurence Bergreen & Sara Fray

Roaring Brook Press

New York

Published by Roaring Brook Press

Roaring Brook Press is a division of Holtzbrinck Publishing Holdings
Limited Partnership

120 Broadway, New York, NY 10271 · mackids.com

Library of Congress Control Number: 2020912183

ISBN: 978-1-62672-122-7

Our books may be purchased in bulk for promotional, educational, or business use.
Please contact your local bookseller or the Macmillan Corporate and Premium
Sales Department at (800) 221-7945 ext. 5442 or by email at
MacmillanSpecialMarkets@macmillan.com.

First edition, 2021

Book design by Mercedes Padró

Picture research by Toby Greenberg

Printed in the United States of America by LSC Communications, Harrisonburg, Virginia

1 3 5 7 9 10 8 6 4 2

To my wife, Jacqueline, and son, Nicholas David

—L. B.

To my husband, Mark Fray, and daughter, Zata Fray
—thanks for your love, support, and inspiration

—S. F.

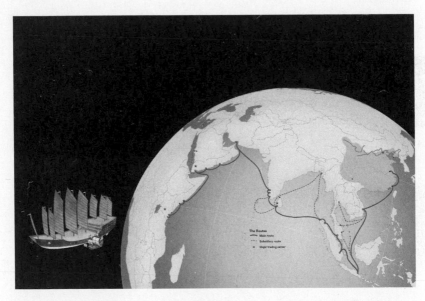

The routes of China's Treasure Fleet, 1405–1433. Side-by-side comparison of one of Zheng He's treasure ships with a ship from the fleet of Vasco da Gama.

Contents

THE PIRATES OF VOYAGE I

The Strait of Malacca was one of the most vital and hazardous shipping channels in the world. To the west lay the Indian Ocean, to the east, the Pacific, and between them were five hundred miles of dangerous waterway teeming with pirates skilled at pillaging ships carrying all the world's goods—spices, gems, fragrances, and silk.

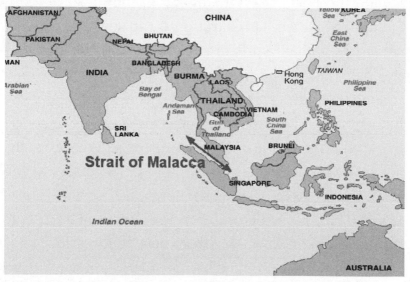

Map of the Strait of Malacca situated between the Malay Peninsula and Sumatra in Western Indonesia.

In the spring of 1407, deep within the dark watery maze of the Strait of Malacca lurked an army of pirates entirely unaware that their reign of tyranny, death, and destruction was about to end at the hands of the seven-foot-tall admiral of the Treasure Fleet, Zheng He.

The emperor of China, Zhu Di, had entrusted Zheng

1

He, his most loyal soldier, with the monumental task of establishing China as the leader of global trade and the ultimate force at sea. Although the admiral preferred peaceful diplomacy to warfare, his fidelity to the emperor drove him to violence. Nothing could stop Zheng He from accomplishing his mission—not even the deadliest, most ruthless army of pirates in the Eastern Hemisphere.

To prepare for battle, Zheng He ordered his fleet to invade the harbor of Palembang in Indonesia's South Sumatra province. Three hundred and seventeen colossal wooden ships spreading massive red-silk sails cut through the murky brown waters of the Musi River. Among them, the smaller vessels, called junks, and the heavily armed combat ships began to swarm the shoreline. Behind them sailed sixty-two gigantic treasure ships adorned with menacing dragon eyes. Spectators at the docks, though accustomed to the usual flow of merchant vessels, had never before witnessed ships of such epic proportions and were awestruck and breathless.

The largest sailboats in the fleet, called treasure ships, were more than 450 feet long, dwarfing anything European explorers would command a full century later. In fact, one treasure ship could fit four of Christopher Columbus's flagships inside it. They were the supertankers of their day and the largest vessels known to traverse the East China Sea or the Pacific Ocean until World War I.

China's Treasure Fleet was more than an armada; it

An imposing Ming treasure ship all but dwarfs a Portuguese ship.

was a well-organized, technologically advanced floating city. There were separate vessels for soldiers, giant
tanks of drinking water, and a vegetable garden. Even
the horses had their own boat. Protecting the fleet were
thousands of heavily armed troops ready to pacify anyone in their way, including the most vicious group of
pirates imaginable.

To secure a future for China's trade route, Zheng
He would have to overthrow the leader of the pirates.
His mission was both imperative and incredibly risky
because local pirates were known to plunder anything
that passed through the Strait of Malacca. The pirates
knew the best hiding spots in the winding waters of
the river inlets, and they used their ambushed victims'
shock to easily board and overwhelm their ships.

The pirate chief, Chen Zuyi, lived like a king. He had amassed an enormous collection of stolen goods, built the largest army of pirates anywhere in the world, and forced the residents of Palembang to obey his violent authority. This created an especially difficult situation for merchants who relied on the city's port to trade for valuable commodities such as black pepper and cinnamon.

⸺

As the treasure ships glided toward the Palembang harbor, imperial troops perched at the tops of the soaring masts scanned the surrounding waterways for pirate activity. The harbor was eerily tranquil; there was no sign of Chen Zuyi or his army, only the steady movement of a small fishing vessel approaching the fleet. As luck would have it, the local Chinese merchant aboard that boat, Shi Jinqing, disembarked with a critical secret: Chen Zuyi and his pirates were hiding in nearby waterways, preparing to ambush the treasure ships. When Admiral Zheng He learned of the scheme, he was left with no choice but to prepare for war.

Wasting not a moment, Zheng He devised a foolproof battle plan and ordered his fleet into a strategic formation. The steady, ominous beating of drums on Zheng He's ships grew louder as flags were raised to signal the ships' launch. The largest ships, with their valuable loads of porcelain, silk, and gold, sailed away from the harbor to block all passages running out to the Java Sea. No one would be able to escape under the watchful gaze of the admiral.

Imperial troops in hundreds of smaller warships readied their swords, explosives, and flaming arrows for a brutal offensive. When all the necessary preparations were ready, Zheng He made the first move.

A small flotilla carrying a messenger traveled across the harbor to demand that the pirate chief surrender peacefully or face the consequences. Zheng He had been warned that Chen Zuyi's surrender was a ploy, and he anticipated his opponent would feign cooperation.

After a brief delay, Chen Zuyi agreed to Zheng He's terms and ordered his fleet of murderers, thousands deep, to gather in the harbor.

How small the pirate ships seemed in comparison to the behemoth treasure ships. Even the Ming Chinese combat ships loomed large over the pirate boats.

Finally, Zheng He gave the signal to attack.

THE ORIGINS OF THE ADMIRAL

Two centuries before the Treasure Fleet was launched, China was the most advanced and populous empire in the world. Major cities in China contained ten times as many people as major European capitals: 750,000 in China's cities compared to the typical 75,000 in cities in Europe.

Monumental statue of Zheng He at Zheng He Park, a prominent historical site in the city of Kunming, Yunnan, China.

China fielded the largest army and navy and maintained the largest trading network in the world, extending its influence across Asia, Indonesia, and India. Although China's wide reach encompassed half the globe, its maritime prowess was relatively unknown throughout Europe.

China was a nation divided against itself and embroiled in multiple civil wars. Ethnic Chinese, Mongols, and Uighur tribespeople fought each other for control of the vast Asian plain.

Beginning in 1206, Genghis Khan, a ferocious Mongol warrior, conquered an expansive region spanning from Mongolia to Beijing. Claiming the peasantry as allies, he attacked the elite of the Jin Dynasty. It is estimated that the battles carried on in his name claimed the lives of forty million people, about ten percent of the population of the world.

By 1251, one of Genghis's many grandchildren, Kublai Khan, had emerged as his successor. During the years of his long reign, Kublai reunified China, and in 1271 he established his own dynasty, the Da Yuan, or "Great Origin," and founded his own capital at what is now Beijing. His realm extended from the Pacific Ocean to the Black Sea, and from Siberia to Afghanistan.

～

This was the changing world into which Zheng He, the future admiral, was born in 1371. His name was originally Ma He, and he spent the first decade of his life in the city of Kunming.

Fourteenth-century Kunming was a teeming center of commerce, with raucous open-air markets brimming with fragrant spices, fresh vegetables, live fowl, leather goods, religious talismans, homemade remedies, and games. It was located in the remote province of Yunnan in southwestern China, surrounded by snowy mountains, algae-infused lakes, and dense rain forests. Yunnan bordered present-day Laos, Vietnam, and Myanmar. Powerful monsoons and a spring wind from the southeast brought humidity and rain to the region. It was 1,700 miles from the Chinese capital, then in Nanjing, and had a culture all its own.

Daily life in Kunming varied greatly from one person to the next. Most of the villagers were farmers or peasants who led modest lives working in the fields, planting and harvesting crops. In the crimson soil—made colorful by its very high iron and aluminum levels— men, women, and children sowed golden wheat, barley, flowers, and pink buckwheat. With a mild, springlike climate, there was red and green as far as the eye could see from flowers and vegetation perpetually in bloom. Village families typically lived in small homes made of wood and stone. Extended family members, including aunts, uncles, cousins, and grandparents, lived under the same roof.

Compared to most other village children, Ma He was privileged, nurtured, and highly educated. The son of a nobleman, he most likely lived in a compound built around a garden, with separate structures for his relatives.

Ma He's family was still loyal to ancient Mongol tradition. By the time of the Yuan Dynasty, millions of Muslims lived in Mongol-controlled territories like

Kunming, where Muslim men held high-ranking positions. Ma He's father, Ma Haji, was said to be a tall and handsome man with a selfless spirit who was respected by the people of his community.

⸻

As a young boy, Ma He spent countless days sitting by the emerald waters of Lake Dian with his elder brother and four sisters. The lake was filled with creaking wooden sailboats searching for golden fish and slippery eels, and the shoreline brimmed with fishermen assembling their vessels. Ma He and his siblings carefully studied the fishermen's boats, committing each part to memory so they could build miniature wooden replicas at home.

On occasion, Ma He's father and grandfather would take the children sailing on the lake to teach them the fundamentals of boating and fishing. It was perhaps on these excursions that they regaled the children with tales of crossing the Indian Ocean to reach Mecca. The men had made the long pilgrimage to the Muslim holy city, four thousand miles to the east in Saudi Arabia, and were called *haji* by the villagers in recognition of their incredible journey.

Ma He's parents were devout Muslims, and religion infused all aspects of the young boy's identity and daily routine. Their family surname, Ma, meaning "Muhammad," served as a tribute to the prophet and founder of Islam.

Islam was first introduced in China around 650 CE by a disciple of Muhammad. Its popularity skyrocketed in the seventh century when Muslim merchants spread messages of faith as they traveled along the prominent network of trade routes, later called the Silk Road, connecting China with the Middle East and Europe.

〜

When Ma He was ten years old, the threat of imperial invasion was imminent. Zhu Yuanzhang, otherwise known as the Hongwu emperor, the founder of the Ming Dynasty, wanted to overthrow the remainder of the Mongol regime along with its rebellious leader, Prince Basalawarmi, whom Ma He's family served in Yunnan.

Unsatisfied with futile attempts at peaceful diplomacy, the Ming emperor commanded his most illustrious general, Fu Youde, to lead three hundred thousand Ming troops to Yunnan and forcibly remove the defiant prince and all his followers. Ma He's father and grandfather were exactly the kind of men Emperor Hongwu hoped to eradicate from his dynasty.

〜

The hand of destiny appeared to reach out and touch Ma He the day General Fu Youde invaded Kunming. The general was traveling along a local road when he came across a ten-year-old boy. He paused to ask the boy if he knew where Basalawarmi was hiding. Loyal to his family and to the Mongol prince, Ma He remarked, "He jumped into a pond."

"Is that so?" said General Fu Youde.

Without warning, Ma He was taken prisoner, as were hundreds of other boys that same day.

In a matter of seconds, Ma He's world filled with darkness and chaos. Ripped away from everything familiar and without his mother, father, or siblings, Ma He found himself lost and alone.

At the time of his abduction, Ma He was probably unaware of his father's fate. Ma Haji was killed resisting the invasion of Ming soldiers and was later memorialized by his son in a tribute. He was thirty-nine years old.

No matter where his captors would take him, Ma He was determined to follow in the footsteps of his venerable father.

As for the Mongol prince Basalawarmi, he was defeated by General Fu Youde, and he took his downfall very hard. He drowned his wife, ordered his ministers to commit suicide, and finally killed himself on January 6, 1382.

⁓

Three years later, Ma He was still a prisoner of war. Like thousands of other young boys from the families of the defeated, he was castrated and joined the ranks of servants of the imperial family called eunuchs. Castration as practiced in China at that time involved cutting off both the testicles and the penis, and many boys died from the procedure or from infection of the wound. It was a gruesome operation performed without anesthesia and without protection from contamination. Only the hardiest boys survived the surgery and entered eunuch life.

Eunuchs were a customary part of imperial China dating back more than two thousand years, to the Han Dynasty (206 BCE–220 CE). Their proximity to the emperor enabled many eunuchs to rise to positions of military and political importance, especially during the Ming Dynasty (1368–1644). Eunuchs lived within the royal residences and worked closely with important government officials, often acting as middlemen between the officials and the emperor. In exchange for their indentured service, eunuchs were guaranteed food, shelter, education, and security. Eunuchs, while critical to the lifestyle of the emperor, were regarded by non-royals as the lowliest of all servants, mostly because of the stigma surrounding their castration.

Within the decorative inner confines of the palace, eunuchs protected and counseled the emperor's courtesans without posing a threat to royal bloodlines and dynasties. Although they could not father children, many eunuchs developed illicit intimate relationships with the women of the court behind the emperor's back.

For the women serving as the emperor's concubines, life was as difficult and fraught as it was for a eunuch. It was isolating, competitive, and regimented, and freedom for many could be found only in death. Part of an ancient global tradition of female slavery, imperial concubines were common in Mesopotamian culture (5000–3500 BCE) and throughout Roman societies of the same time period (27 BCE–476 CE.)

In China, it was customary for the emperor to keep, in addition to his empress, a harem of concubines to increase his dynastic longevity by fathering more children. More sons meant more heirs to the imperial throne. The majority of the Ming emperors' concubines were forcibly taken. Young girls recognized for their beauty were scouted by court officials and abducted from their homes. Like eunuchs, they had to live in the palace and adhere to the strict regimen of imperial life.

The rest of the concubines were girls offered by their own parents for service. Some underprivileged families took their daughters to the emperor to relieve the financial burden of raising them, while some wealthy aristocratic families strategically placed their daughters in the imperial court to advance their own political agendas.

Women of the imperial harem were organized by rank according to the strength of their relationship with the emperor. The more the emperor favored a concubine, the higher she rose. The most influential woman was the empress, who traditionally hailed from the most powerful family in China. She alone was respected as the emperor's one true wife. Beneath her were the highest-ranking consorts, who controlled the daily lives of those of lower rank. The concubines were isolated within the palace grounds, and communication with the outside world was strictly forbidden.

Concubines were required to conform to strict height and weight guidelines and had to master the skills of dressing, walking, and behaving properly. Most crucially, they had to pass a hygiene test without the help of perfume or deodorant. The ladies of the court conducted regular inspections of the concubines, and if they did not pass these tests, they were disgraced and dismissed from court.

Like so much else in the royal court, life was a competition. Concubines were forced to compete against one another to capture the emperor's attention and affection. All of them were bound by the astrological calendar that determined which woman could be intimate with the emperor on any given day. A woman's selection depended on the date, time, and circumstances of her birth—all designed to be in accordance with the wishes of heaven. Some concubines waited for years for their chance, and some were never chosen.

The acclaimed Yongle emperor surrounded by women of the imperial harem.

Outside of the harem, eunuchs handled a multitude of tasks. They arranged the affairs of the imperial household and kept the inner workings of the administration secret from the public. They taught their masters about court etiquette, formal dining, and sexual intimacy. They supervised construction projects, military equipment, weapons, and provisions. To carry out these critical functions, many eunuchs formed their own elite societies. As Ma He came of age, seventy thousand eunuchs were busy serving the emperor.

During the Ming Dynasty, attending to the minutiae of the emperor's daily life depended entirely upon the service of his eunuchs. Everything from timekeeping to bathing was carefully ritualized, with eunuchs performing specific tasks at precise moments of the day. Upon waking, eunuchs would rush into the emperor's bedroom to change his chamber pot and offer him silken toilet paper. Bathing, grooming, and dressing were other elaborate rituals managed by eunuchs from the Department of the Bathhouse and the Directorate of Royal Clothing.

For the emperor's sustenance, hundreds of piping-hot delicacies like hand-pulled noodles, spiced meats, and salted fish were constantly being prepared for him to select. Before any of the food met the emperor's lips, a eunuch would insert a silver needle to test for arsenic. If the food was poisoned, the needle would, in theory, become discolored. As a last line of defense, a chosen eunuch would consume a small amount of the same dish to test for poison in case the needle failed to detect it.

To transport their master throughout the palace grounds, burly eunuchs would carry him in a sedan, an elaborately ornate covered throne set upon long wooden carrying poles. The emperor was hand-delivered to all of his various buildings, day or night, rain or shine.

Eunuchs castrated as young boys were called *tong jing*, or "pure from childhood," and they were typecast as effeminate and emotionally fragile. Everything about Ma He flew in the face of this cliché. He grew into a robust man, extremely tall and masculine in all respects except the ability to have children. According to one early description, he was "seven feet tall and had a waist about five feet in circumference . . . he had glaring eyes and a voice as loud as a bell."

After several years of education and eunuch training, Ma He was assigned to the household of the prince of Yan. Ma He and the prince, despite their religious and social differences, developed an unusual rapport and friendship. Although the prince was royalty and the eunuch was fated to a life of subordination, each had a transformative effect on the other's career. The two men were eleven years apart in age—Ma He was thirteen years old and the prince twenty-four when Ma He joined the household—but together they plotted the prince's path to the throne of China. In a dangerous world, each depended upon the other for survival. The prince became Ma He's most important sponsor, and Ma He, in turn, helped to make the prince among the most significant emperors ever to rule China.

THE EMPEROR

The prince of Yan, Zhu Di, was the fourth son of the Hongwu

The Yongle emperor, ruler of the Ming Dynasty from 1402–1424.

emperor. Born in 1360, he was known as a talented soldier, tall, handsome, athletic, and clever. Thanks to his father's indulgence, Zhu Di enjoyed a loving, supportive childhood and was educated by some of the most prestigious scholars in China. He learned about his culture's history through the examples of his ancestors. Accomplished princes of the past had had a strong moral center, and Zhu Di looked to emulate them by surrounding himself with people who were loyal, honest, and modest.

Despite his advantages and good company, Zhu Di was exceedingly restless and ambitious. He had been trained as a soldier and wanted to help his father by spearheading imperial military campaigns. Recognizing his son's spirit and talent, the emperor gave Zhu Di his first assignment: Yunnan province.

It was a blood-soaked campaign that ripped apart families and annihilated thousands of Mongols and non-Chinese tribesmen, but for the prince, it was a victory. As a reward, Emperor Hongwu sent Zhu Di to Beijing to live in his own palace and rule the city. His sole responsibility was to protect his principality from Mongol invasion. Zhu Di now had hundreds if not thousands of his own eunuchs to serve and protect him. One of them was Ma He.

———

At the prince's residence, Ma He stood apart from the rest. Physically, he towered above his eunuch counterparts, and he had long limbs and penetrating eyes. Ma He exuded an air of upbeat confidence, steadfast loyalty, and unmitigated respect for his new master. His upbringing had served him well, and the qualities instilled in him by his father shone through like an inextinguishable fire.

Ma He became one of Zhu Di's most important bodyguards and servants. Wherever the prince went, Ma He was close behind. Zhu Di was constantly carrying out military campaigns for his father, and so Ma He, out of necessity, became a toughened soldier. Ma He would spend his adolescence at war against the Mongols, proving his loyalty to the prince who had replaced his family's legacy of Mongol service.

Instead of the traditional comforts of palace life, Ma He and the prince became accustomed to the rigors of military camps. They lived like nomads, moving from camp to camp on assignment from the emperor.

As soldiers, their association overrode the traditional barriers between servant and master, eunuch and prince. On the battlefield, they were brave comrades in arms fighting for their lives, with the survival of each depending entirely upon the other's judgment and skill.

⸺

On June 24, 1398, Zhu Di's father, the Hongwu emperor, died at the age of sixty-nine. Hongwu had wanted his favorite son, Yiwen, to succeed him, but Yiwen's death in 1392 had forced the emperor to reconsider a successor. He had to choose between Zhu Di and the continuation of Yiwen's line in Hongwu's twenty-one-year-old grandson, Zhu Yunwen. The emperor's corrupt advisers saw the opportunity for a power grab and persuaded the emperor to choose the less experienced candidate, Yunwen.

Hongwu's sons were very upset by the emperor's decision, and to prevent a civil war from breaking out, they were forbidden to attend his funeral in Nanjing. Shortly after the ceremony, the new emperor, Zhu Di's nephew Yunwen, began a controversial plan to seize power from all the remaining princes to ensure that he was the only legal authority.

As a result, Zhu Di witnessed many of his brothers imprisoned in their own homes. The princes were callously stripped of not only their authority, but also their armies and their dignity. One of Zhu Di's brothers, Zhu Bo, set his own palace on fire, burned his family, and committed suicide. Zhu Bo chose to sacrifice everything rather than be imprisoned by the newly appointed emperor.

A year into Yunwen's reign, Zhu Di was the only prince left posing a threat to the throne. The emperor, eager to annihilate the last stronghold of resistance, sent a small military force to arrest two of Zhu Di's commanders on false charges. Resisting their request, Zhu Di lured the militia into his palace and executed them. The struggle between Zhu Di and his nephew had escalated to new heights.

To determine his next move, Zhu Di looked inward. After much introspection, the prince realized he had no choice but to avenge his brother Zhu Bo and overthrow the emperor. But first, he would appeal to his nephew, now known as the Jianwen emperor, in writing:

"My five young brothers . . . have all in the space of a few years been stripped of rank and forcibly removed [from their positions] . . . [Were] a benevolent and sage [ruler] on the throne, how could he endure this?"

The Jianwen emperor dismissed Zhu Di's urgent concerns. By now it was apparent that the only way to rid

China of the emperor, a puppet of his Confucian advisers, was to overthrow him. It was time for an uprising.

The revolution began quietly. Zhu Di assembled a group of eight hundred soldiers, who gathered in secret to train in the palace park. To disguise the sound of the military exercises, they filled the park with squawking geese and ducks. Meanwhile, the soldiers drilled day and night.

Surprise raids soon became the norm in the capitals Beijing and Nanjing. For every attack Zhu Di and Ma He orchestrated against Nanjing, the Jianwen emperor answered with an assault on Beijing.

~

This situation took on new importance in 1402, when an influx of dissenting eunuchs from Nanjing arrived in Beijing. Ma He had spread the message that the eunuchs of Beijing were treated well and valued for their skills and service. Mistreated by the inexperienced new emperor, the eunuchs of the imperial court in Nanjing rebelled and fled to aid Zhu Di in his stronghold.

The rebel eunuchs met with the prince and provided him with secret military intelligence. They revealed all the defensive weaknesses of the capital, ensuring that Zhu Di's men could penetrate the palace. To ready himself for the new offensive, Zhu Di employed Ma He as one of his top military commanders.

First, Zhu Di and Ma He ordered the secret army to cut off the delivery of provisions to major cities. Next, following the advice of the imperial eunuchs, they attacked the cities that had inadequate defense systems, passing over the ones that were well fortified. City by city they approached Nanjing, eventually surrounding the capital. But conquering the capital would be by far the most difficult military challenge Zhu Di had ever faced.

Nanjing was protected by fifteen miles of thirty-six-foot-high walls. Guards lived inside the claustrophobic chambers of the wall, and any guard who abandoned his post was immediately beheaded. The guards' mission in life was to defend their post by making the gate completely impassable.

However, like the imperial eunuchs, the palace officials were unhappy with the Jianwen emperor and had begun distancing themselves from him. When Zhu Di and his army arrived at the outskirts of Nanjing, two disgruntled royal commanders met with the prince to strike a deal. The city, palace, and throne would soon belong to Zhu Di.

On July 13, 1402, Zhu Di, commander Ma He, and their army marched victoriously through the Jinchuan Gate. As if by magic, the guards had disappeared, and the massive structure had opened to admit Zhu Di. The unhappy palace officials had delivered the capital.

Zhu Di and his troops found the palace engulfed in fire; the scorched corpses of the empress and her six-year-old son were recovered, along with the remains of a man of about Jianwen's age. It appeared that the emperor had died in the blaze—but had he really? Zhu Di declared that the body, burned beyond recognition, must be that of his rival for the throne, Jianwen, and asserted that he, Zhu Di, and he alone, was emperor. And yet . . .

A rumor was whispered that a strange monk had been spotted fleeing the fire. Some believed the emperor had come into possession of a map of secret passageways that ran beneath Nanjing. He was said to have shaved his head and disguised himself as a Buddhist monk to make his escape, but not before ordering the palace burned to the ground with his family inside.

The Jianwen emperor never reappeared, and Zhu Di's fears never came to pass, but his suspicion, however unlikely, would haunt Zhu Di for the rest of his days. It symbolized perhaps a manifestation of the guilt and unworthiness he felt upon seizing the throne. He was a usurper, and the label clung to him like a curse throughout his life.

—————

Zhu Di officially ascended to the throne on July 17, 1402, and declared himself the Yongle emperor, the name meaning "perpetual happiness."

As heaven's appointed rulers, emperors enjoyed vast powers over the lands they governed. The Yongle emperor drew his omnipotent authority from a political ideology formulated in 1046 BCE called the Mandate of

Heaven. The mandate formally recognized the founding member of the Zhou Dynasty, King Wen, and each of his successors as the son of heaven. According to the doctrine, all emperors of China were chosen by ancient divine forces to govern Earth on their behalf. While a king had absolute authority over a single territory, the emperor of China had divine authority over all of China as the son of heaven. Throughout Chinese history, the emperors were all men with a single exception, Wu Zetian, a politically gifted and capable empress who shattered precedents and founded her own dynasty in 690 CE.

The Yongle emperor, with his reputation as a usurper, was almost as revolutionary a figure. Despite his name, his first act as emperor was anything but jubilant: He systematically purged the men from within his own administration who subscribed to his nephew's old system. Confucian officials and military personnel who had persecuted Zhu Di during his reign as prince of Yan were hunted down, tortured, and executed.

Yongle also publicly announced that the years during which his nephew had held the throne were inconsequential and that his own reign was the rightful continuation of the era of his father, Hongwu. To support his claim, he ordered the falsification of palace records to expunge the reign of his nephew, the Jianwen emperor, from all imperial documents. It was as if Zhu Di's predecessor had never existed.

In 1403, the Yongle emperor embarked upon a radical political quest to transform China into the largest global superpower of the fifteenth century. To begin, Zhu Di encouraged private trade, and facilitated commerce by permitting valuable commodities such as spices and gold to be traded freely. His Confucian advisers, who based their view of China's economy on indigenous agricultural pursuits, were aghast when the emperor went a giant step further by encouraging foreign merchants to come into the country to trade. Two of his declarations reverberated across the length and breadth of the Middle Kingdom: "Now all within the Four Seas are as one family" and "Let there be mutual trade at the frontier barriers in order to supply the country's needs and to encourage distant people to come."

The emperor felt the time had come for all neighboring lands to recognize China as the wealthiest and most powerful empire in the world, and that a naval fleet of unparalleled size and technology would be just the right symbol to deliver this intimidating message of leadership. Emperor Yongle theorized that all the surrounding southern and western ocean regions could be pacified into accepting China's rule with the right naval force. Even more, he reasoned, the subservient nations would benefit from the relationship because China offered protection and prosperity through the promotion of peaceful economic trade and military support.

In return for the exportation of Chinese luxury commodities like porcelain and silk to India, the Malay

Peninsula, and Africa, the emperor anticipated a flood of foreign leaders presenting their finest treasures as gestures of their appreciation and subservience. Thus installed as sovereign of global trade, Zhu Di would legitimize his reign as the rightful son of heaven and erase his standing as a usurper.

To turn this revolutionary theory into reality, Emperor Yongle gave the edict for the launching of the first Treasure Fleet in 1404. Construction of the immense ocean fleet began immediately in the shipyards of Nanjing.

Meanwhile, the emperor rewarded his friend and loyal eunuch, Ma He, with the honor of becoming admiral of the Treasure Fleet. Ma He, who had never led an ocean expedition, was now in charge of the greatest and most intimidating armada in existence.

A ceremony in honor of the newly anointed admiral was held on February 11, 1404. Ma He was officially given the surname Zheng—meaning "prosperity" or "government"—and was also awarded the honorary title of grand director. As grand director and commander of the Treasure Fleet, he was now the highest-ranking eunuch in China, and he wore a red robe to distinguish himself from the lower-ranking eunuchs, who were attired in blue.

As Zheng He's star rose, the floating city took shape in the shipyards of Nanjing.

CONSTRUCTION

Fifty thousand years ago, sailors from Asia journeyed across the Pacific Ocean on rafts made of bamboo to colonize New Guinea and Australia. Later, people from north of the Yangtze River traversed the Bering Sea land bridge and settled on the North American continent. These pioneers were the ancestors of the first Native Americans.

From 3000 to 2500 BCE, the people of southeastern Asia voyaged across huge expanses of water, including the Indian and Pacific Oceans, to reach the African and American continents.

As China's oceangoing prowess continued, emperors commissioned expert navigators to search the seas for distant lands with medicinal herbs or, better yet, the secret elixir for immortal life.

Emperor Qin Shi Huang sent Xu Fu in 219 BCE to search for the elixir that could confer immortality. Xu Fu sailed across the seas with a crew of three thousand aboard sixty ships. According to legend, he sailed all the way to Japan and discovered Mt. Fuji, where he remained for the rest of his days.

Zheng He's treasure ship with nine masts.

At the dawn of the fifteenth century, the Ming Dynasty under Emperor Zhu Di sponsored astonishing innovations in shipbuilding and employed technology advanced beyond anything that would appear in the West for centuries. In only three years, from 1404 to 1407, no fewer than 1,681 ships were constructed to fulfill numerous imperial directives. While that number is impressive, the Chinese had long enjoyed a rich maritime tradition as mariners and shipbuilders.

Under the direction of Zhu Di and his newly appointed admiral, Zheng He, the Treasure Fleet's enormous vessels were about to make history. Zheng He would command 317 ships and a crew of almost twenty-eight thousand. The mighty armada dwarfed its European successors.

Global Explorers of the 15th and 16th Centuries	Ships	Crew
Zheng He (1405–1407)	317	27,800
Christopher Columbus (1492–1493)	3	90
Vasco da Gama (1497–1498)	4	170
Ferdinand Magellan (1519–1522)	5	257

The Treasure Fleet's enormous vessels were assembled on the waters of the Qinhuai River in their own specialized shipyard called the Treasure Shipyard. The Treasure Shipyard was part of a network of shipyards in Nanjing called the Longjiang Shipyards, which swelled during Yongle's reign to accommodate the frenzied activity.

Fifteen-hundred-foot-long dry docks were sectioned off from the waters of the river by high barriers. When the ships were ready to sail, the barriers were removed and the docks would fill with water, allowing newly completed vessels to float into the river.

The shipyard employed a massive assemblage of workers. There were as many as thirty thousand: sailmakers, shipwrights, carpenters, caulkers, ironsmiths, rope makers, timekeepers, and men responsible for the horses hauling materials around the yards. The first in command, Zheng He, likely visited the shipyards, accompanied by a retinue of eunuchs, to ensure that all the preparations ran smoothly.

Within Zheng He's imperial fleet, sixty-two of those ships were 480-foot-long treasure ships. Other vessels included 339-foot-long horse ships built to transport horses, 257-foot-long supply ships for food and water, 220-foot-long combat vessels for troop transport, and 165-foot-long warships designed for fighting and weaponry.

Built to withstand whatever hazards the sea would offer, the treasure ships and their accompanying flotilla were designed to combat the forces of nature. One of the biggest problems sailors encounter when spending long periods of time at sea is running out of basic supplies like drinking water. To avoid this perilous pitfall, the master craftsmen built special tankers large enough to provide water for the twenty-eight thousand sailors for an entire month.

Starvation was also not of pressing concern thanks to the ingenious creation of floating gardens; these were ships filled with soil and growing plants to sustain the crew. To maintain precious reserves of live fish caught at sea, the daily catch was kept alive in tanks inside the hulls of the treasure ships.

The dimensions of the ships were determined by numbers having conceptual significance. The length of the treasure ships, as recorded in imperial documents, was 444 *chi* (*chi* being a unit of measure equal to around 13 inches, or a little more than 1 foot) to represent the following concepts: China as the "middle kingdom" set amid the Four Seas, Earth with four corners (as was the geographical belief of the time), and the four seasons.

To ensure that such massive structures would be seaworthy, shipbuilders used various types of wood for specific parts of each vessel. Demand for lumber became so great that the coastal supply of trees was exhausted, necessitating the creation of a large inland lumber operation located on the outskirts of the Yangtze and Min Rivers. After the trees were felled, the timber was gathered and floated downstream on the Yangtze—the longest river in China—to the shipyards. Ten thousand tung trees were planted on the mainland to provide oil and textile fiber for the fleet, and local ironworks grew and grew to provide the necessary pots, pans, nails, and other iron tools and implements.

The demands of equipping the fleet were so great that the resources of the entire nation were stretched to the breaking point. In addition to timber, the massive ships required great quantities of silk, candles, and oil, not to mention provisions, anchors, and rigging.

Outfitting the crew was also laborious, with officers requiring ceremonial robes adorned with the imperial dragon, the symbol of national might. Factories sprang up overnight to produce them according to strict specifications. The robes necessitated a special weave called cut silk, which revealed the design on both sides; it was finer than that used in the celebrated French Gobelins tapestries of the seventeenth century. Weavers who could not meet the high standard of the cut-silk work faced punishment and even prison.

It was not long before the local population providing

goods and services began to feel the burden, and to complain. In theory, they would eventually benefit from their hard work, when the ships returned laden with spoils and treasures, but in reality, the abundance collected by the fleet on its voyages would go directly to enrich those in Zhu Di's court. The people, on the other hand, faced higher taxes and corrupt officials in the country's quest to build the fleet.

———

As villagers and craftsmen tirelessly toiled, the emperor and his admiral proudly surveyed the skeletons of the massive structures in the Nanjing docks. The first major component of the boats assembled was the hull. The hull of a ship is the watertight main frame of the vessel, within and on top of which other structures, like decks and masts, are built. The Treasure Fleet's vessels' hulls were constructed with the durable wood of elm, camphor, cedar, and sophora trees.

Treasure ships had double hulls, where a second hull was built inside the first hull to create separate watertight compartments. The space within the hull was not only excellent for storage; when the hull was doubled, it also made the ship virtually unsinkable in the face of giant waves or ramming by other ships during warfare.

The hulls were given a V-shape with a razor-sharp point in the style of a traditional *fuchuan* ship, designed to cut through the rough waters of the South China Sea.

Within the hulls, the treasures carried by the ships could be safely stored. Up to 2,500 tons of cargo could be secured within each treasure ship. Massive quantities of expensive silks, porcelain, cotton, iron, salt, hemp, wine, candles, and tea were stockpiled for trade with foreign countries.

Inside the inner hull were the bulkheads, the upright walls that separate the chambers of the hull. The ships' seaworthiness was greatly enhanced by the bulkheads, which mimicked the internal cavity of a bamboo stalk.

The ingenious bamboo-stalk design made the ships almost unsinkable because each bulkhead chamber was a separate watertight compartment, so the entire hull of the ship would never flood. Even if a few bulkheads were breached, the rest would remain dry. It would be more than three centuries before European ships incorporated bulkhead technology, long after it was known in China.

―――――

In addition to watertight bulkheads, proper weight distribution ensured the safety of the vessel. Because the treasure ships were so wide, achieving stability at sea was critical. Shipmakers gave the ships a long keel and heavy ballast to equalize the weight on all sides.

Another way to create equilibrium at sea was with massive floating anchors weighing over a ton each. These could be cast off the sides of the ships when needed.

Further stabilizing the ships were balanced rudders placed in front of and behind the sternpost, making the ships easier to steer. Rudders are essentially a vessel's fins under the water. In the case of the treasure ships, they were thirty-five-foot-long beams made of elm and mounted to the bottom of the ship.

The rudders determine the direction of the vessel by redirecting the water flow. When the rudder is turned using a wheel or tiller on deck, the water strikes it with more force on one side and less force on the other, moving the vessel in the direction of the lesser pressure.

The rudders, while massive, were also adjustable to avoid fracturing the hull on rocks or in shallow water. Varying depths of the ocean, such as unexpected shallows, were not a problem for the Ming Chinese armada because their rudders could be raised and lowered efficiently. The adjustable rudder was another example of a Chinese maritime invention that would be adopted in the West much later—a thousand years later.

⁓

Each treasure ship had nine masts carrying twelve square sails made of red silk. The sails were hoisted into position with a pulley system controlled by the crew on the deck.

The treasure ships were four tiers high, soaring hundreds of feet above the waterline. The lowest deck was filled with dirt and stones for weight. The second tier was devoted to the luxurious living quarters designed for Zheng He, the eunuch directors, and the foreign ambassadors. The next level up, the third tier, consisted of an outdoor kitchen and a bridge for sailors to operate the pulleys for the sails and anchors. The fourth

Interior of a Ming Chinese treasure ship, including its cargo space, upper deck, and captain's quarters.

deck, which partially covered the third deck, was a high platform dedicated to combat.

The exteriors of the treasure ships were embellished with carvings of dragon heads, phoenixes, and eagles. The ships were painted with brightly colored designs, including dragon eyes on the prows. The lower hulls were decorated with illustrations of the sun and moon. But as stunning as the ships' exteriors were, the interiors were even more remarkable.

The opulent living quarters of the grand cabins of the Treasure Fleet featured polished wood floors and elegant railings. The cabins were trimmed with gold and had their own balconies. Abundant colorful silks, fine porcelain pieces, and other valuable goods might have decorated each room. The grand cabins of the treasure ships were exquisitely outfitted for the kings, queens, and other dignitaries they were expected to ferry across the seas.

The accommodations for the thousands of ordinary

seamen were much more basic—nothing more than a bedroll. The sailors themselves came from the lower rungs of society; most of them were criminals for whom a strenuous life at sea was slightly more desirable than prison. They were also swayed by the promise of generous rewards of money and fabrics upon their return. If the sailors were harmed or died at sea, the emperor would pay their families for their loss.

Surprisingly, there was also a sizable contingent of elderly women, whom Zheng He hired to repair the clothing and footwear of the twenty-eight thousand sailors. While details of the seamstresses' living conditions are generally unknown, it can be assumed that they, too, slept on deck or in simple bunks.

———

Remarkably, by 1405 more than three hundred pristine vessels stood ready to sail on the Yangtze River. The sheer size of the fleet was awe-inspiring, even to the builders who had created the ships, and the anticipation over the maiden voyage reverberated throughout the entire mainland.

On the eve of the first voyage, the emperor threw an opulent banquet in honor of his longtime friend Admiral Zheng He and his crew. There was an abundant feast laid out on endless tables bearing roasted pigs and goats, rice, pastries, and wine.

As a gesture of his gratitude, Emperor Yongle presented tributes. Zheng He and the other highest-ranking eunuch officials were given gold. Captains, astrologers, geographers, and other important personnel were awarded silver, and the remainder of the crew was presented with silk.

To safeguard the sailors from calamity on the journey, the emperor, Zheng He, and all in attendance presented sacrifices and enthusiastically recited prayers to the sea goddess, Mazu, often referred to as Tianfei ("princess of heaven"), one of her formal titles. The goddess was embraced in Chinese maritime culture as the celestial patron of sailors and fishermen. She was known for her ability to perform miracles to save the lives of seafarers.

Tianfei (or Mazu), the goddess of the sea, protectress of seafarers and fishermen. Tianfei's influence was so widespread that many temples across China and Asia are dedicated to her.

The protectress of our ships, the Celestial Consort, brilliant, divine, marvelous, responsive, mysterious force, protector of the people, guardian of the country. "Come down one and all to this incense feast; partake of this sagely vessel. Come riding on auspicious clouds from the ends of the earth. Come down and grace our incense table. Let us seat you in your respective places and carefully prepare a pure goblet that we might reverentially offer the immortal masters a flagon of wine, beseeching them to protect our ships and valuables."

Tianfei's spirit, attired in a red dress, drifted above the ocean, directing sailors away from harm. Her dual spirits could help even desperate sailors in the most isolated waters of the four oceans. One spirit had a thousand eyes that scanned the vast waterways, and the other had supremely delicate ears able to hear everything on the ocean wind. She attained a cultlike status throughout Fujian and coastal China.

Another universal belief was that giant dragons lurked in the sea and held sway over waterfalls, rivers, and oceans. Each of China's Four Seas was represented by its own dragon king, and sailors offered wine to those dragons to gain their favor and win their protection.

When this day at an auspicious hour we set down the compass needle, let the dark water dragons go down into the sea and leave us free from calamity.

After the feast, prayers, and sacrifices, Admiral Zheng He readied his crew for the epic journey ahead.

VOYAGE I

Admiral Zheng He (1371–1433), China's greatest maritime explorer and renowned diplomat.

Outward Bound

In the fall of 1405, 317 gleaming ships lifted their anchors and drifted away from the shipyards of Nanjing. The maiden voyage of the Treasure Fleet was finally underway.

Aboard the ships, twenty-eight thousand men attended their posts, performing various tasks to keep the floating city running smoothly. Robust sailors hauled on the ropes of the pulleys that hoisted giant red square sails that rose high above the decks. The navigational experts carefully watched the floating needles in their magnetic compasses to ensure that the ships set out upon the right course. Burning incense sticks tracked the passage of time on the massive wooden decks. Flags were raised to communicate messages within the fleet, and bells and gongs also signifying various nautical directives reverberated off the serene waters of the Yangtze River.

Commanding this complex group of magnificent vessels was the emperor's most trusted brother-in-arms, Zheng He. The admiral had only one fear: failing the emperor. If Zheng He couldn't establish China as the leader in global commerce, Zhu Di could sentence the crew to death to save face, or, worse, imprison their families. The question of national pride constantly hung over Zheng He's head. This was, on one hand, a commercial voyage designed to import the riches of the world to China, but at the same time, it was a voyage meant to intimidate and subdue the surrounding world with China's prosperity and might.

There is no reason to think that Zheng He undertook his responsibilities for the sake of material gain. He was motivated by his devotion to Zhu Di. Summing up the anxieties of his crew, Zheng He wrote, "Our one fear is not to be able to succeed." The reputation of the Yongle emperor, the Ming Dynasty, and China's global identity rested heavily upon the broad shoulders of commander Zheng He.

Astonishingly, this was Zheng He's first significant naval assignment. Despite his lack of seafaring experience, the emperor had chosen him to lead the fleet because of his lifelong devotion, military talent, and spiritual complexity. Zheng He was a Muslim, a Buddhist, and a worshipper of Tianfei, and therefore he was well prepared to handle the diverse religious matters sure to arise abroad.

Zheng He's close relationship with the emperor also helped to elevate the status of his fellow eunuchs, ensuring that the eunuch class held power at sea. Leading the fleet were seventy eunuchs ranked in importance from directors or ambassadors of China down to junior directors and their assistants. The most powerful grand director was Zheng He. He was in possession of blank scrolls stamped with the emperor's seal, giving him the ability to issue orders in the emperor's name and ultimate authority over his massive crew. Zheng He alone decided the fate of his men and the course China would take in foreign lands, whether it was live or die, attack or flee, sink or swim. The admiral used his power at sea to fulfill the political vision of his master, the emperor.

Zheng He and his advisers had thought of just about everything when it came to personnel. Caring for the well-being of the crew was one physician for every 150 men. Also on the medical staff were pharmacologists to collect herbs and other important substances used as medicines and elixirs in foreign countries.

The armada included officers who enforced protocol at banquets, as well as foreign-language translators to aid in communicating with local populations. The Treasure

Fleet was well prepared to represent the glory of the Ming Dynasty under all imaginable circumstances.

—

The gravest obstacle Zheng He faced was pirates. The Treasure Fleet was transporting extremely valuable cargo in massive quantities, making the ships vulnerable to looting and plunder. To prevent a pirate attack, the thousands of troops in the armada were armed and ready to protect the haul of the treasure ships. They and their impressive surplus of weapons filled the combat ships of the fleet. Most of the soldiers and sailors were criminals who had been banished from China. Ruthless and tough, they had nothing to lose.

Ninety-three military commanders directed the troops, and supervising the commanders were eunuch officials. And to stanch threats from within such as mutiny, each ship's captain was granted the imperial authority to decisively deal with offenders.

The crew scanned the seas, looking for signs of pirates by day and by night. Nighttime was the more threatening period. Under the cover of darkness, pirates could emerge seemingly out of nowhere and steal aboard the ships, and by the time the crew realized what was happening, it would be too late. And so the troops stayed vigilant at all hours.

To enable troop transportation on land, the horse ships carried mounts so soldiers could easily mobilize. Other specialty ships were filled with materials needed to make repairs at sea. Workmen of many types, including ironsmiths, caulkers, scaffold builders, and sail makers, traveled aboard these vessels.

While Zheng He charted the course for the expedition, it was up to the ships' pilots and their crews to manage the minutiae of navigation and timekeeping.

Navigating the armada was a complex task handled by an official astrologer, whose knowledge of the constellations helped to guide the ships. There was also an official geomancer, who foretold the future by studying the geographic features of handfuls of dirt. They made navigational decisions in tandem by studying the constellations with the aid of a key Chinese invention: the compass. The magnetic compass first emerged in China in the fourth century BCE, and crude early models reveal those devices relied on naturally magnetic lodestone pointers. By the fifteenth century, the Chinese compass was comprised of a magnetic needle shaped like a fish that floated in a small bowl of water. The fish-shaped object would slowly align itself in a north-south position, enabling the pilots to set a course. This simple device made the long-distance exploration of the Treasure Fleet possible. Thanks to the compass, nights without stars became navigable. The fleet could sail around the clock if need be. It would be another century before European explorers employed similar technology.

As for time, it was measured with incense clocks. Sticks of incense were placed in holders with special markings attuned to their rate of combustion. As the incense stick burned down, notches on the clock indicated how much time had passed. Incense clocks were preferable for ocean travel because of their simplicity and sturdy nature, and for the fact that they were far more reliable than weather-dependent solar clocks.

A ship's speed could be estimated by throwing an object in the water at the bow and tracking its movement to the stern while chanting a timekeeping rhyme.

To determine their location, captains studied a twenty-one-foot-long sailing chart that illustrated significant landmarks and geological features, including mountains, beaches, rivers, hazardous undersea rocks, and shorelines.

―――

To launch the emperor's trade initiative, the fleet first made for the city of Calicut in the fall of 1405. A market town famous for its prized spices on the southwest coast of India in the state of Kerala, Calicut was regarded as the most important port in South Asia. Its merchants supplied traders with black pepper, worth its weight in gold, and other spices like ginger, turmeric, and cardamom, as well as rare species of wood. It was the ideal place for the Treasure Fleet to begin establishing China as the major player among wealthy traders in the region.

The fleet continued southward along the Chinese coast for four hundred miles, toward the mouth of the Min River. They arrived at a large, bustling harbor on the Fujian coast, still within the borders of China's empire, to make final preparations before heading out to sea.

Zheng He and his crew spent the next several months loading the ships with food, drink, and additional supplies as well as making repairs to the ships. To catch favorable winds for the journey, Zheng He knew they had to wait for the winter monsoon, set to arrive in late December and early January.

During the months of limbo, Zheng He paid tribute to the Buddha and the deity Tianfei at the local temples. He also renamed the port Taiping, meaning "peaceful"—a fitting name for a tranquil harbor that allowed sailors to prepare for strenuous adventures at sea.

After weeks of worshipping in Buddhist temples nestled high in the mountains around Taiping, Zheng He had an epiphany. He realized he could help his fleet safely exit the harbor by transforming the shrines situated atop a mountain into a signal tower. From the vantage point of the pagoda, Zheng He could survey the entirety of the harbor and deploy specially decorated flags to direct his armada. The fleet could then communicate his orders to one another.

One fateful day, by the order of the admiral high above the harbor, a symphony of multihued lanterns, ringing bells, and beating drums signaled to the crews to hoist the anchors and sails. The time had finally arrived to leave the safety of China's shoreline and traverse the South China Sea.

As the winds picked up, Zheng He's massive fleet moved swiftly away from the Min River to face its first navigational challenge: a cluster of large rocks known as the Five Tiger Passage. Zheng He and his navigators would have to carefully maneuver the armada through the rocky obstacle course to reach the Formosa Strait, which separates the Chinese mainland from what is now Taiwan, an island nation of fourteen thousand square miles. Zheng He ordered that the ships' thirty-foot-long rudders be lifted to avoid unexpected shallows and rocks, and he gingerly led his ships through the difficult passage.

After clearing these hazards, the fleet sailed south-southwest into the Formosa Strait, which presented dangers of its own. The strait ran for more than a hundred miles, and in the deepest areas, the water was no longer the blue or green of shallower waters but inky black, and the currents ran in unpredictable directions. But it seems that Zheng He negotiated these challenges without difficulty, thanks to the seaworthiness of his huge ships and the long experience of his crew.

The southern end of the strait led toward the South China Sea, one of the Four Seas that were believed to border ancient China in each of the four cardinal directions. The West Sea was an enormous saline body of water known as Qinghai Lake (the largest lake in China), the East Sea was the East China Sea, the North Sea was

Lake Baikal (the largest freshwater lake in the world), and the South Sea was what the Treasure Fleet called the South China Sea.

～

After enduring ten days of wind-fueled ocean swells, the weather-beaten fleet arrived at the tropical coast of Champa near modern-day Quy Nhon, Vietnam, about 1,400 miles south of Nanjing.

While aesthetically pleasing, with palm-thatched homes and blooming vegetation, Champa was a war-torn kingdom in a perpetual state of violence. Many of the fishermen moonlighted as pirates and smugglers, profiting from the local trade. Admiral Zheng He understood that Champa could be dangerous, but he also knew how valuable a relationship with its king and merchants would be for China.

The Treasure Fleet was a well-fortified militarized armada with the capacity to pacify a region like Champa to permit peaceful trade. The sheer size of the treasure ships, the massive accompanying flotilla, and the enormous crew could intimidate even populations practiced at waging war. While the people of Champa regularly welcomed large foreign merchant ships, they had never witnessed a spectacle like the Treasure Fleet.

Disembarking from the flagship, Zheng He and a retinue of eunuch ambassadors traveled inland, across what is now Laos, to meet with the local king. King Jaya Sinhavarman V was a devout Buddhist who, according to one of the fleet's chroniclers, Fei Xin, donned a "three-tiered elegantly decorated crown of gold filigree."

Unlike the rest of the population, who lived in squat, simple palm-thatched huts, the king maintained a regal home constructed of wood, bricks, and tiles. The royal residence towered above those of the peasant population, whose modest huts were outfitted with entryways that were no more than three and a half feet in height. Out of reverence for the king, the monarch's subjects always bowed their heads when entering or exiting their homes.

Wearing white clothing was a privilege reserved solely for the king; everyone else sported black, yellow, or purple attire. Men and women pinned their long hair neatly in buns at the backs of their heads. Everyone, including the king, was barefoot.

Rhinoceroses, water buffalos, and elephants were plentiful, and local merchants often sold animal trophies such as horns or teeth to foreign merchants. Despite the glaring cultural differences between the Ming Chinese and the Cham, as the people of Champa were called, and the political strife of the region, Zheng He and the king came to an understanding that would enable peaceful and profitable trade to flourish. Zheng He had successfully secured the first major port along China's new trade route, and the hulls of the treasure ships filled with valuable goods from the region.

The Cham favored Ming porcelain, which Zheng He traded for durable ebony, fragrant lakawood, and

calambac incense. As parting gifts of tribute, the Cham people gave the Ming emperor elephants' ivory tusks, elephants' teeth, and rhinoceroses' horns.

A mid-fifteenth-century porcelain and cobalt jar decorated with winged animals, including a horse and a horned deer, most likely inspired by the Treasure Fleet under the direction of Zheng He.

And with the promising start to the journey, Zheng He instructed his crew to ready the fleet for their next trading port, the immense volcanic island of Java.

After enjoying several days of favorable winds, the Treasure Fleet reached the sprawling sea empire of Majapahit in Java and sailed on to Gresik, on the northeast coast of the island.

While anchoring the ships in the unremittingly hot climate, the fleet encountered a sizable community of affluent Chinese merchants who had settled in the region at the end of the fourteenth century, during Emperor Zhu Yanghang's travel embargo. To the travelers' surprise, a thousand Chinese families were thriving in thatched-roof huts.

The hamlet was ruled by a man from China's

Guangdong province. Inside their humble shelters, everyone sat and slept on grass mats. The local inhabitants were quite wealthy due to the steady flow of foreign trade, having amassed significant quantities of gold and precious stones.

There Zheng He and his crew sampled a delicacy called *mang-chi-shih* (in English, mangosteen), a fruit that resembled a cross between a pomegranate and an orange but had a tart taste. They observed that the locals ate with their hands and constantly chewed areca nuts (also called betel nuts). The nuts are similar to tobacco, having a stimulating effect.

During the flurry of trading spearheaded by Zheng He and his ambassadors, members of the crew disembarked from the ships to explore Gresik. They watched in awe as an epic duel between two local warriors unfolded. First, the competitors, holding long bamboo stalks filed to a razor-sharp point, circled one another to the rhythm of beating drums. As the drumbeat intensified, the warriors moved dangerously close to one another, thrusting the tips of their bamboo spears into their opponent's flesh. The deadly game continued until the wives cried, "*Na-la, na-la!*" Traditionally, if a combatant died from a wound inflicted in a duel, his wife would be given to the victor as a trophy, while the rest of his grieving family was compensated for its loss with a single gold coin.

There was also a remarkable funeral ritual reserved for the town's devout Hindu upper-class population.

When a Hindu man of high standing died, his body was cremated. The man's wives adorned themselves with vibrant flowers, decorative grasses, and colorful cloth and mounted a wooden platform above the cremation pyre. Swaying and proclaiming, "In death we go with you," the women dropped themselves into the fire to let it consume their own living bodies along with the dead body of their master.

⸻

When the trading was complete, Zheng He and his men departed for the next stop on the route to Calicut. Sailing north along the coastline of Sumatra, the admiral ordered his fleet to bypass Palembang and continue toward Atjeh (now spelled Aceh). Circumventing Palembang, the most significant independent region in Sumatra, proved to be a clever military maneuver.

Palembang's harbor was strategically situated along the natural chokepoint of the deadly Strait of Malacca, which connects the South China Sea and the Indian Ocean. From northwest to southeast, the Strait of Malacca steadily narrows until it is only forty miles across and a mere ninety feet deep. Because ships passing through the strait were generally trading vessels loaded with precious goods, the waterway had become a hot spot for pirates to plunder vulnerable cargo.

With Palembang destabilized because of the ongoing conflict between Java and Sumatra, ruthless Chinese pirates had formed to create a shadow government. Chen

Zuyi, who hailed from Guangzhou, became the leader of these rebels and outcasts, who transferred their loyalty from China's emperor to Chen Zuyi. The pirate chief plundered any ship that dared to pass through his domain, assisted by thousands of fishermen turned pirates who overwhelmed trespassers and murdered their crews.

Aware of the danger, Zheng He decided to sail past Palembang Harbor, knowing he would have to subdue the region on his return journey to China. To ensure safe passage for future Treasure Fleet missions, Zheng He had to vanquish the pirates' stronghold, but for now, he would secure peaceful trading along the rest of Sumatra's coastline and move on to the island of Ceylon (now called Sri Lanka).

—

When the ships of the Treasure Fleet arrived in Ceylon, they were met with outright hostility. The king, full of pride, was not intimidated by the Chinese ships or their weapons. He insisted that the foreigners leave his land immediately and even threatened the admiral's life. While Zheng He could easily have overwhelmed the region with his destructive weapons and superior manpower, he chose a more calculated approach and directed his crew to prepare for departure. This was not the moment to challenge Ceylon, he decided; that would come later.

Before departing, Zheng He and his men spotted an impressive collection of gems that were common in the region, including brilliant rubies, sapphires, and pearls. They also visited the fabled holy footprint of the Buddha at the top of a lofty mountain at the center of the island.

As the ships lifted their anchors, Zheng He might have wondered whether his failure to pay tribute to the Buddha had angered the king. Perhaps this religious oversight was at the core of the king's enmity.

Drifting away from the shoreline of Ceylon, the admiral commanded his massive fleet to sail onward.

～

After three days, the Treasure Fleet rounded the southern point of India and finally arrived at Calicut, in present-day Kerala, on the southwestern coast of India. The fleet laid anchor, and Zheng He and his crew were warmly welcomed into a sophisticated trading society.

For centuries, Jewish, Arab, Chinese, and Phoenician people had journeyed to Calicut to trade black pepper and other valuable spices, along with textiles. Calico, a textile made from unprocessed cotton, originated there, so its name most likely comes from that of the city.

Zheng He and his men regarded Calicut as "the great country of the western ocean." The port allowed all ships passing through to trade and take on provisions such as food and water. The types of foreign goods circulating in Calicut varied according to which of the region's two annual monsoon seasons it was. During the favorable season for western trade, when the prevailing winds came from the southwest, valuables from the regions around the Red Sea and Persian Gulf would flood the market. Eastern trade from Sumatra and the Malay Peninsula dominated during the opposing monsoon season, when the winds generally came from the northeast.

Calicut's Zamorin society was divided into four distinct classes. The upper class was composed of Hindu Brahmin priests and warriors, while Muslims ran the trading operations. In fact, Muslim propagation of Islam throughout the region can be traced back to its followers' critical role as masters of trade who spread their message of faith while managing valuable merchandise. The third class, below Muslims, were wealthy property owners, known as the Chetti class. Fishermen and divers comprised the lowest class.

Like the Ming Chinese, the Zamorins maintained an army, a navy, and a system of law and order. A minor offense might be punishable by cutting off a hand or foot, while a serious crime would result in the confiscation of property and execution of the offender and his or her entire family.

HOMEWARD BOUND

The Treasure Fleet idled in Calicut from December 1406 through April 1407 to wait for the favorable monsoon winds and trade their large stash of valuables

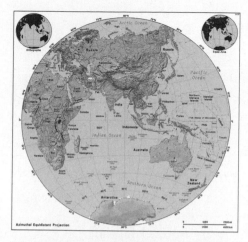

Map of the Eastern Hemisphere depicting everything east of the prime meridian (0 degrees longitude), including Europe, Asia, Africa, and Australia.

for locally sourced pearls, coral, gemstones, and coveted black pepper. When the monsoon winds shifted to the southwest, Zheng He and his men readied the fleet to travel back across the Indian Ocean toward China. They would journey home to the emperor with an impressive haul of foreign goods and objects of tribute. In addition, envoys from Calicut, Quilon, Semudera (in other contexts spelled Samudera), Delhi, and Malacca joined the Treasure Fleet to serve as ambassadors for their respective kings and to deliver gifts.

Zheng He had successfully secured the first segment of China's trade route, dutifully furthering the emperor's quest to establish China as the wealthiest, most powerful nation on earth. But there were still the lingering threats of pirates and the perils of open-ocean travel.

To ensure the expansion of the trade route and the success of subsequent Treasure Fleet voyages, Zheng He had to overcome a crucial obstacle. He would have to sail into the harbor of Palembang and defeat Chen Zuyi, who ruled the area. For almost a decade, the pirate chief had plagued the Strait of Malacca, raiding any vessel he desired, and no one had dared to threaten him. His pirates knew where to hide until conditions were right to assault their victims; their knowledge of the local geography, coupled with their overwhelming numbers, made them appear to be an unstoppable force.

In the spring of 1407, the Treasure Fleet approached the harbor of Palembang. As the sailors released the chains to drop the thousand-pound anchors, troops huddled in the crow's nests at the tops of the soaring masts and scanned the waters for Chen Zuyi's pirates.

The admiral designed a foolproof battle plan. He began by moving his ships into a strategic formation. By placing the treasure ships and their valuable cargo farthest from the shore, Zheng He secured his assets and blocked the passageways leading to the open sea. The admiral was now ready to lure his victims into a manageable battleground.

And so, he made the first move.

A small Chinese flotilla traveled across the harbor of Palembang with a messenger asking for Chen Zuyi's surrender. Zheng He had been warned by Shi Jinqing that Chen Zuyi would pretend to surrender so his men could ambush the fleet.

After a brief delay, the pirate chief agreed to Zheng He's terms and ordered his fleet of pirates, thousands deep, to emerge from their clandestine waterways.

Zheng He's immense treasure ships, manned by enormous crews, towered over the minuscule pirate boats. After the pirates had left their hiding places, Zheng He gave the signal to attack.

Chinese troops deployed "sky-flying tubes" that spewed gunpowder and burning fragments of paper onto the pirates' sails. Next came an assault with "fire bricks" and "gunpowder buckets," which were grenades made of paper saturated with poison.

Each bit of ammunition that landed on the pirate ships' decks set the vessels on fire, creating toxic smoke and flames. The pirates gasped with every breath of poison they inhaled.

As the hours passed and the battle raged on, Treasure Fleet troops launched thousands of flaming arrows onto the sails of the pirate ships, turning the harbor into an inferno. But all of this was merely a prelude to the violent ramming of the combat ships into the fragile hulls of the wooden pirate ships.

As the sky grew dim with the waning daylight, flames licking at the brigands' ships illuminated the silhouettes of Treasure Fleet troops in fierce combat as they launched deadly grenades filled with shrapnel at their enemy. Adding to the chaos was smoke from the poisonous chemicals and flaming human excrement hurled onto the decks of the pirates' ships by the men of the encircling Chinese flotilla. Pirate ships' sails burst into flames and fed the fires on board, sending crew after crew to their watery graves. The fighting continued well into the night and for days, even months, after that.

Chen Zuyi and his pirate army had finally met their match, and their flimsy ships were systematically destroyed. The sheer size of the Treasure Fleet, its ample supplies and forces, and Zheng He's brilliant strategic maneuvering had delivered a hard-fought victory.

At the end of the battle, the pirate chief himself was captured and his ankles were bound with heavy chains. Chen Zuyi was placed in a cell aboard one of the treasure ships, where he was guarded for the remainder of the voyage. The admiral would leave the fate of Chen Zuyi in the hands of the emperor.

Ten pirate ships had been burned, seven ships had been captured, and five thousand pirates had been killed. The pirates' reign over the Strait of Malacca was finally over.

Zheng He was now the most powerful naval commander in Asia.

——

The mighty armada now faced its next challenge: the return trip to China over vast stretches of the ocean in ships laden with dignitaries, prisoners of war, precious spices, gold, and incense along with a crew of twenty-eight thousand, plus horses and other livestock. Despite all that Zheng He had already achieved, his fleet's safe passage back to Nanjing was critical. If any of his ships, especially the treasure ships, were lost at sea, Zheng He would be viewed as a disappointment, and all of the successive expeditions would be canceled. Even worse, his crew would be dishonored and executed, and their families on the mainland would be imprisoned or banished.

Zheng He knew that the emperor would support subsequent Treasure Fleet missions only if the first mission was successful. To reap the rewards of his journey, Zheng He had to return to the docks of Nanjing with his armada in first-rate condition.

As the fleet set out across the South China Sea, the astrologers, navigators, and meteorologists worked together to determine if there would be any bad weather. They unrolled the twenty-one-foot-long chart, carefully examined the floating fish-needle compasses, and, at

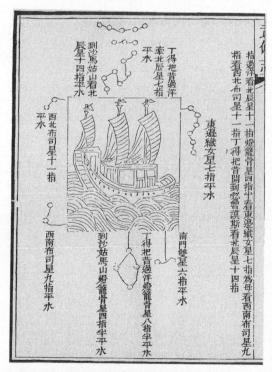

A reproduction from 1628 of a map, or star chart, as it was called, employed by Zheng He's Treasure Fleet during its voyages from 1405–1433.

nightfall, stared intently at the constellations in the sky. Staying on course meant facing less trouble, because the quicker they arrived at the Nanjing harbor, the less likely they were to fall victim to storms, rocks, or mighty sea dragons.

One evening, without warning, the sky darkened. Clouds blanketed the ships and a drizzle turned into a steady soaking rain. The downpour intensified and the waves began to swell. Zheng He and his crew found themselves trapped in a typhoon. Their enormous ships lurched in the rising seas. Waves broke over the decks, soaking man and beast as the ships heaved like so many giant toys, but the vessels did not sink, thanks to the watertight bulkheads.

Fear over rumors of a belligerent sea dragon lurking beneath the ocean gripped the crew, who believed the thrashing of its giant body and tail were surely to blame for the turbulent sea. As mighty as the treasure ships were, the crew knew they were no match for a creature capable of sending ships to the ocean floor.

Remembering the prayers that Zheng He had asked his crew to dutifully recite, the men called out to Tianfei, goddess of the sea, for assistance. Thousands of desperate pleas to the goddess reverberated off the wooden decks of the ships as lightning repeatedly crashed into the masts. The waves were as tall as the tops of the towering masts of the treasure ships, and the wind and rain were blinding.

Zheng He must have been wondering if all would be lost when, "as swiftly as an echo . . . there was a magic lantern in the mast and as soon as this miraculous light appeared, the danger was becalmed . . . There was [now] nothing to fear."

Tianfei had rescued the crew, and the men cried out in gratitude. Thanks to the crews' prayers, the tempestuous storm had passed.

The "magic lantern" they saw was actually a naturally occurring phenomenon called Saint Elmo's fire, in which glowing plasma (ionized gas) hovers on the masts of ships during stormy weather. It appears when a lightning-filled atmosphere creates an electrical field around a tall object like a ship's mast, resulting in a luminous apparition.

For a crew as spiritually minded as Zheng He's, this spectacle, in combination with the calming weather system, came as a sure sign of deliverance by the goddess Tianfei. Zheng He believed that he and his men owed their lives to Tianfei's protection, and he was determined to demonstrate his gratitude to the goddess who had rescued them.

After the Treasure Fleet docked safely in Nanjing on October 2, 1407, Zheng He recounted the miraculous tale of Tianfei's intervention to the emperor and implored him to grant Tianfei a symbolic title of

A bas-relief commemorating the arrival of Admiral Zheng He during his voyages of exploration.

honor—and so the emperor did. With Yongle's blessing, Tianfei came to be known as the "protector of the country and defender of the people."

⁓

The maiden voyage of the Treasure Fleet was a triumph of Ming Chinese naval power and technology. Zheng He had successfully overseen construction of the most impressive armada in history and had traversed the Indian Ocean and South China Sea while keeping his fleet intact. The trade route he had established from Champa to Malacca, Java, Sumatra, and finally Calicut set the navigational model for the next six voyages.

What next? For the Yongle emperor, the next step was to remove political threats. Without hesitation, the emperor ordered the swift, public beheading of Chen Zuyi. Surely the story of how the notorious pirate chief lost his head would reverberate throughout the Four Seas as a warning.

With Chen Zuyi gone, the Strait of Malacca was no longer a den of pirates, and China's trade route was primed for expansion.

VOYAGES II & III

One of the many temples dedicated to the goddess Tianfei.

VOYAGE II, OUTWARD BOUND

In October 1407, immediately following the return of the maiden voyage, Emperor Yongle issued the edict for the second voyage. Thousands of laborers swarmed the docks to prepare forty-nine treasure ships for the upcoming expedition in 1408.

Beyond the horizon, far off the coast of mainland China, the Treasure Fleet glided along its newly established trade route without its most illustrious crewmember. Admiral Zheng He remained in China to attend a grand ceremony held on January 21, 1409, in honor of the goddess Tianfei. The admiral credited Tianfei for delivering him from the grip of the ferocious sea storm on the maiden voyage. In gratitude, he oversaw the repair of Tianfei's resplendent temple at Meizhou, Putian, in Fujian.

The shrine rose on a hillside overlooking the shipyard and the Yangtze River. (It was rebuilt in 2005 and still evokes the serenity surrounding worship of the Sea Goddess.)

Zheng He adorned the temple with trees from faraway lands, as well as ornaments fashioned from silver and gold. Within it, pungent incense wafted through the air, and the walls reverberated with murmured prayers.

Zheng He installed a total of seven stone tablets—called steles—throughout the Eastern Hemisphere to memorialize the tale of his seven ocean voyages. One of the steles was placed in Tianfei's temple by Zheng He himself, and its inscription urged the emperor's subjects to be sincere and loyal to the goddess. If they were, it assured them, all their prayers would be answered. Above the tablet, murals decorated the temple walls with episodes from the goddess's life. There were depictions of her in the supposed year of her birth, 960, of her realization at sixteen that she had the power to heal the sick, and her death in 987.

As the cult of Tianfei proclaimed, a successful sea voyage, especially one as ambitious and risky as those undertaken by the Treasure Fleet, required collaboration between the human and the divine.

~~

In the open sea, hundreds of miles from Tianfei's temple, the Treasure Fleet separated into two squadrons led by Zheng He's eunuch appointees Wang Jinghong and Hou Xian. One group headed south toward Vietnam. Among the thousands of men aboard those ships was a chronicler named Fei Xin. He was only twenty-two years old and was avidly curious, and he kept a record of the customs the fleet encountered that he found noteworthy. Fei Xin sailed with the Treasure Fleet on four of the seven voyages, compiling a detailed account of each journey.

Zheng He had also recruited a twenty-five-year-old Muslim Arabic translator named Ma Huan to join the fleet. Ma Huan hailed from Hangzhou Bay, which was a center of navigation. Bred for life at sea, Ma Huan became an invaluable translator and the main chronicler of the Treasure Fleet voyages. While Ma Huan took a special interest in the religious customs he witnessed, Fei Xin focused on the diets and living conditions of the populations he encountered.

When Fei Xin disembarked in Vietnam and had a chance to look around, he remarked that the principal chief reminded him of a "decorated Buddhist guardian made of clay," especially as he rode above the throng atop an elephant, followed by five hundred soldiers carrying spears, swords, and javelins.

When the Ming Chinese arrived in force, the chief ordered his elephant to kneel, and he dismounted. He and his men approached respectfully and fell to their knees, crawled forward, and lay prostrate at the feet of their guests to give and receive tributes.

They exchanged elephants' teeth and rhinoceroses' horns, along with a medicinal aloe considered so precious that "the one who secretly steals and sells it will have his hands cut off."

~

As the days wore on, the hot and humid climate oppressed the Treasure Fleet sailors, who were accustomed to cooler, drier air.

Despite the weather, the ship's chronicler, Fei Xin, became fascinated by the indigenous cuisine. He described Vietnamese wine as a mixture of rice and medicinal pills that were poured into earthenware jars and stored for long periods of time to breed maggots. When Fei Xin sampled it, he enjoyed "an excellent liquor" through a four-foot-long bamboo straw. Winemaking also involved collecting gall—a fluid secreted by the liver. The gall was mixed with wine and sometimes used for bathing as well, Fei Xin reported.

He also took note of how different the daily schedule of the local population was from his own. Most people stayed in bed until noon, indicated by the beating of a drum, and they did not go back to sleep until after midnight. When the moon appeared, he wrote, "they drink wine and sing and dance to celebrate it." Life in

Vietnam was unlike anything Fei Xin had witnessed before.

〰

A separate Treasure Fleet squadron, under its own imperial directive and headed for Calicut, docked in Siam (modern-day Thailand) to gather supplies and trade with the locals. Siam's tropical topography was stunning, with tall mountains and swampy valleys.

As the ships laid anchor in the translucent waters, the crew was greeted by an all-female group of merchants. The female traders supplied the ships with wood and ivory. The merchants, like the rest of the women of Siam, were the matriarchs of the society. Strong-willed, intelligent, and extremely independent, women ran all the cultural touchstones in Siam.

Men were subservient to their female counterparts, with daily affairs and business matters being managed solely by women. Even the king, the ruling force of the land, left punishment and trade decisions entirely in the hands of his wife.

The crew's dealings in Siam came to an abrupt end when word arrived of Zheng He's proximity. Without hesitation, the fleet hoisted its crimson sails, exited the harbor, and made for Java. It was finally time for the squadrons of the fleet to reunite under the leadership of Zheng He.

〰

Off the coast of volcano-riddled Java, the fleet was finally a single unit once again. Zheng He, who had sailed from

China to rejoin his crew, was embraced by his eunuch brothers as their one true leader.

While the admiral attended to imperial affairs with local rulers, chronicler Fei Xin learned about Javanese political folklore. He recorded a fable about a "devil in the sky" who merged with a "water monster with a black face, red body, and red hair" to produce one hundred offspring, all of whom went on to consume "human blood and flesh." The water monsters nearly wiped out the entire population, but then a bolt of lightning suddenly shattered a rock, and inside the rock sat a man who became the country's ruler, saving the people from the monsters.

—

Back at the Javanese shoreline, Zheng He soothed inflamed tempers. The bitter history between his country and Java needed resolution, and now was the time for Zheng He to flex his diplomatic muscles.

During Kublai Khan's reign, two generals had been dispatched to lead an army to subdue Java, but their campaign coincided with a drought. Without water or food, Fei Xin recounted, "the soldiers were at their wits' end. The generals, Shih Pi and Kao Hsing, prayed in this manner, 'If Heaven gives us water, we shall live, if not, we shall die.' They struck their spears into the ground, and a spring miraculously emerged. The soldiers drank their fill of the sweet water." When they had recovered, Shih Pi and Kao Hsing sent their troops into battle against the Javanese. "More than a hundred thousand foreign soldiers were routed," according to Fei Xin. The soldiers killed them and advanced inland, and as they went, they "cooked and ate them." Although this was most likely untrue, the story of this infamous deed had provoked the Javanese to claim the Chinese were cannibals.

The rancor had not ended there. Between 1401 and 1406, more than one hundred personnel at the Chinese embassy were put to death. But when Java learned that in response China was readying an enormous army and demanding an apology and payment of sixty thousand ounces of gold, it quickly complied with all the conditions. The dispute came to an end, but China continued to be wary of Java.

Now, with the arrival of the Treasure Fleet, Zheng He adopted a different approach—bestowing gifts upon local leaders, their families, and the people of Java. As a result of his generosity, the country began to "enjoy heaven's blessings," and the Javanese king attributed the subsequent plentiful harvests and absence of strife on his island to Zheng He's visit. In gratitude, he sent emissaries to China to offer memorials and presents. Zheng He had conquered Java by means very different from the one chosen by the earlier generals: generosity and pacification.

Java, too, was now under the umbrella of China's hegemony.

Voyage II, Homeward Bound

Along the route back to Nanjing, the fleet paused at an archipelago in the Andaman Sea known as the Similan Islands, off the southern coast of Siam. The scene was one of primordial beauty, with a glistening sun over pristine beaches. But while the views were aesthetically remarkable, the Treasure Fleet sailors did not go there to unwind from the voyage.

Instead, Zheng He sent government troops onto one of the islands to cut incense. According to Fei Xin, they came back with six large logs "whose aroma was pure and far-ranging. The pattern [of the wood] was black, with fine lines."

While there, the visitors attracted attention. Fei Xin described how "the people of the island opened their eyes wide and stuck out their tongues in astonishment, and [they] were told that 'We are the soldiers of the Heavenly Court, and our awe-inspiring power is like that of the gods.'"

The Treasure Fleet coasted back into Nanjing in the summer of 1409. Within months, the ships were prepared to embark upon their third voyage to the Indian Ocean.

Voyage III, Outward Bound

The fleet once again quit the docks of Nanjing in October 1409. The grand director, as Zheng He was called, had become by far the most important admiral in China's history. He was confident in his ships and knew his crew could handle their vessels with matchless efficiency.

With forty-eight ships and thirty thousand men, the admiral's itinerary for the third Treasure Fleet voyage included the Strait of Malacca, the site of his infamous pirate battle with Chen Zuyi, as well as its bustling trading port. After employing peaceful diplomacy there, Zheng He would continue to the hostile region of Ceylon to pacify the local king.

Cutting through the waves, Zheng He and his crew braved the vast open waters of the Indian Ocean, southwest of China. In the fifteenth century, to be master of the ocean was to be master of the world, or most of it. Oceans account for about seventy percent of Earth's surface. The Indian Ocean is the third largest on the planet, after the Pacific and the Atlantic Oceans. It covers about fourteen percent of the world's surface, or 26,463,000 square miles, with an average depth of about thirteen thousand feet.

In Zheng He's time, the Indian Ocean's islands were almost all uninhabited, its azure waters unspoiled by human meddling.

Into the pristine waters the Treasure Fleet sailed with Zheng He in command, along with his trusty adjutants, Wang Jinghong and Hou Xian. The first stop was the Fujian coast, north of Hong Kong and west of Taiwan. The fleet proceeded along a southerly route toward Champa, as Vietnam was known, and Temasek, an archaic name for Singapore, arriving at last at the important trading post of Malacca, to the northwest, in Malaysia. It was here that Zheng He attended to an important diplomatic assignment.

—————

Malacca is believed to have been established in 1377, when a ruler known as Parameswara, or "king," founded a new realm after fleeing an attack by the Javanese Majapahit Empire. Seeking protection from his enemies, Parameswara traveled to China to pledge his loyalty to the Yongle emperor. For this gesture, he paradoxically received a seal of recognition of the independence of his kingdom. The China-Malacca alliance infuriated Parameswara's jealous neighbors to the north, in Siam, and they confiscated the seal.

When Zhu Di heard about this outrageous thievery, he sent the Treasure Fleet to convey a replacement seal to Malacca and reaffirm the alliance forged with Siam on the previous voyage. At the same time, the Ming Chinese hoped that the pact would warn the Javanese, in the south, that the Treasure Fleet was not to be trifled with.

Hot, humid, flourishing, and inviting, Malacca was fast becoming a vital trading post in China's expanding commercial sphere. Thanks to its strategic location, soon Arabs, Persians, Jews, Tamils, Bengalis, and other traders would converge there to do business with one another.

The Tamils and Bengalis specialized in cloth; the

Arabs and Persians looked for goods from China; and the Ming Chinese dealt in camphor, silk, and porcelain. Still other tribes traded in gold, black pepper and other spices, sandalwood, and rice. Ma Huan left this eyewitness account:

Malacca was a well-established city surrounded by a palisade with four gates and watch towers. Inside the walled towers was a second fortification, a kind of citadel, within whose confines were the merchants' warehouses, the treasury, and food storehouses. The Malacca River divided the city into two almost equal halves, the southern half being the inner citadel and the ruler's compound and the northern half, reached by a bridge some distance from the river mouth, containing the residents of many foreign merchants. The bridge and its approaches comprised the main venue for all commercial kinds. Constructed on the bridge was about a score of market stalls: an easy location for small watercraft to reach with their loads of produce and also close to the docks where foreign sea-going vessels unloaded goods for shipment.

Upon arriving in booming Malacca, Zheng He presented himself not as a conqueror, but as a petitioner interested in fortifying Parameswara's fledgling regime. To demonstrate his goodwill and generosity, the admiral presented the king with a pair of silver engraved seals, a ceremonial cap, and a royal sash. Most impressively, Zheng He erected a stele that proclaimed Malacca and the surrounding region a sovereign nation—one that now owed its continued existence to China.

Zhu Di had supervised the writing of the text that would appear on the stele. It was one of only four times that the emperor authorized the Treasure Fleet to export a stele, the others going to Japan, Brunei, and Cochin (now called Kochi). This monument represented a symbolic conquest—and a projection of might that would protect and benefit Malacca.

"We think the great service that wise and virtuous rulers render for heaven and earth," the stele read, "is that their governance defines and aids the working of heaven, earth, and humanity, assists the forces of nature, and molds the myriad things so that the sun, the moon, and the stars shine." Zhu Di continued in this exalted manner, concluding the stele with a poem addressed to the "people of ten thousand generations to come."

Posterity will smile upon your deed as time passes; and your sons and grandsons will have limitless good fortune.

Henceforth Malacca would be "treated as a subject state of the Middle Kingdom in order to excel and to be distinguished from the barbarian domain." The high-flying rhetoric concealed a serious strategic purpose.

Potential rivals, especially the warriors from Siam, grudgingly acknowledged that they had been overwhelmed and outsmarted by the Chinese newcomers. Trade, not military might, was king.

Zheng He's fleet bartered for valuable items, especially durable ebony, medicinal aloe, and tree resin, which doubled as caulking.

〜

On closer examination, life in Malacca was not as ideal as it seemed from afar. The longer Zheng He's men spent in Malaysia, on this and subsequent voyages, the more involved with the Malays they became.

Malaysian spiritual philosophy encompassed Buddhism and Hinduism as well as ancient folklore. Zheng He's men discovered that the Malays lived in an animistic universe. They believed that a spirit or soul dwelled in each person, in each animal, and even in objects such as houses, boats, and trees, and that these spirits were easily insulted. Treat rice grains roughly, they believed, and the rice would have its revenge by refusing to grow.

The people of Malacca lived in fear of tigers, and not just the beasts in the world, but also men who they believed turned into tigers and preyed on pregnant women, whose blood they could detect from miles away. They imagined that somewhere inland, these tiger ghosts inhabited huts fashioned from the hair of women. These beliefs influenced Zheng He's crew, some of whom thought they saw men turning into tigers and tigers turning into men, so they learned chants designed to keep the tigers away. "Take away thy cat," they implored the spirits. "Harm not, nor destroy my body!"

Zheng He's men stuck close to harbor rather than risk exploring the depths of the jungle, where anything could happen to them.

〜〜

It was with a sense of relief that the crew of the Treasure Fleet departed Malacca and its hazards, traversed the strait at its narrowest point, and arrived on the island of Sumatra. Even greater rewards and challenges than those in Malacca awaited the visitors on the island. A land of natural wonders, Sumatra provided camphor, frankincense, ginger, black pepper, and medicinal herbs in profusion. There was also sulfur to be collected in proximity to the island's active volcanoes. In fact, Sumatra had more than its share of terrifying eruptions, earthquakes, and monsoons. It also boasted rhinoceroses, elephants, and red-haired orangutans.

The visitors braved them all to collect more items believed to have medicinal properties. The fleet included no less than 180 medical personnel, who collected panaceas such as rhinoceroses' horns to treat snakebites; sulfur for a variety of afflictions, including rheumatism; deer antlers to strengthen bones and improve potency; and chaulmoogra-seed oil, considered an effective treatment for leprosy.

And there was more to add to this rare and wonderful pharmacopoeia—cloves, benzoin, putchuck (a fragrant root), and, perhaps most important of all, incense to repel mosquitoes and thereby avoid the debilitating illnesses they carried. As soon as the medical personnel collected the herbs, spices, and roots, the men set about boiling and drying them to preserve them for the voyage home.

———

As the Treasure Fleet cruised northward beyond Sumatra, the ships called on various islands, none considered more idyllic than tiny Pulau Rondo, ringed with a coral reef, at the northernmost extremity of Indonesia. "This island floats beautifully on the surface of the sea," Fei Xin rhapsodized. "Waves beat it and clouds dance upon it. Every time that spring arrives, crowds of dragons gather and couple on the island, leaving behind their spittle."

By *dragons* the young sailor likely meant sperm whales, and *spittle* was referring to their ambergris, a product of their intestines. Ambergris was prized by the Chinese and the Arabs, who associated it with dragons and dealt in it as both medicine and perfume.

Fei Xin was eager to examine it at close range. "This dragon-spittle is like fat or glue; it has a blackish-yellow color and intensive fishy smell. After some time, it comes to form large lumps of mud. Sometimes it is cut out from the belly of a huge fish." And, "when burnt, it gives out a clear incense, most delectable. The price is not cheap." He proceeded to quote prices in various local currencies to illustrate its value, concluding that it is "extraordinarily expensive," particularly in China.

—

The fleet's next stop was the legendary ancient civilization of Ceylon. According to Western legend, Ceylon was God's recompense to Adam and Eve for losing the Garden of Eden. It was one of the first countries to establish a hospital, and this had been a thousand years earlier, in the fifth century. Ancient merchants knew Ceylon as the source of cinnamon, among the most valuable of all spices. Over time, Ceylon maintained ties with the Roman Empire. When Cleopatra sent her son Caesarion into hiding, one of the places he was said to have headed for was Ceylon. Several hundred years later, in 429, Buddhist monks could be found in Ceylon. The area later became renowned for its engineering marvels, such as reservoirs.

By the time Zheng He, Fei Xin, and the Treasure Fleet crew arrived, Ceylon was past its prime, and murderous local politics threatened to engulf the visitors. The region was also embroiled in a three-way civil war as Hindus and Tamils battled Muslim insurgents for religious dominance.

Zheng He was determined to pacify the region after the blistering hostility he had encountered there on the maiden voyage. He carried with him an unusual tablet meant to mollify the citizens with its message written in Mandarin, Tamil, and Persian. The multiplicity of languages demonstrated Zheng He's sophisticated approach in dealing with multicultural populations, as well as his appreciation for and understanding of the three religions practiced by the Ceylonese.

The Mandarin section featured reverence for the Buddha: "Deeply we do revere Thee, Merciful and Honored One, of bright perfection wide-embracing, whose Way and virtue passes all understanding, whose Law pervades all human relations, and the years of whose great kalpa"—eons—"rival the river-sands in number." The tablet announced that the fleet was coming with a sense of great respect, rather than for conquest. "We . . . now reverently present before the Lord Buddha, the World-Honored One, oblations of gold and silver, gold-embroidered jeweled banners of variegated silk, incense burners and flower-vases, silks of many colors . . . in order to manifest the high honor of the Lord Buddha. May His light shine upon the donors."

The Tamil section expressed the same sentiments to the Hindu deity Tenavari-Nayanar and praised Allah and the saints of Islam.

Zheng He took care to offer tributes of gold, silver, silk, perfumed oil, and superbly crafted glossy ornaments to each of the gods in the same amounts so that no one would be offended. Following the ceremony, local leaders took turns offering the admiral Ceylon's indigenous goods—until a defiant political newcomer named Alakeshwara caused a disturbance.

Alakeshwara boldly announced to the admiral that

he would not pay tribute or allow a multilingual tablet to be erected. A bitter feud between Zheng He and Alakeshwara ensued. Zheng He would not tolerate any disrespect toward his emperor, the son of heaven, or allow Ceylon to disrupt the flow on China's trade route. The time had come to consider options beyond peaceful diplomacy.

The situation took a drastic turn for the worse when Alakeshwara dispatched his son to demand gold and silver from the Chinese. But Zheng He refused to trade with anyone who denied the emperor his tribute. Alakeshwara retaliated by sending fifty thousand men to capture Zheng He's forces, felling trees to block their route back to the safety of the ships.

Keeping his wits about him, Zheng He realized that with Alakeshwara's troops scattered throughout the jungle, the capital itself would be deserted. Zheng He led a battalion of men numbering only two thousand into the city, where they proceeded to Alakeshwara's headquarters. They captured Alakeshwara and spirited him onto one of the ships. Eventually they took him to Nanjing to face the judgment of Zhu Di himself, who decided to pardon the troublemaker and return him to Ceylon.

This heroic version of events was commemorated by the Ming scholar and historical compiler Yang Rong, who portrayed Zheng He's bravery as the absolute peak of the Treasure Fleet's achievements. "Straight-away, their dens and hideouts we ravaged," he wrote, "and made captive of that entire country." And, in even harsher terms:

Bringing back to our august capital,
Their women, children, families, and retainers, leaving not one,
Cleaning out in a single sweep those noxious pests, as if
    winnowing chaff from grain...
These insignificant worms, deserving to die ten thousand times
    over, trembling in fear...
Did not even merit the punishment of Heaven.

In a show of mercy, matters took a different turn:

The august emperor spared their lives,
And they humbly kowtowed, making crude sounds and
Praising the sage-like virtue of the imperial Ming ruler.

Another Ming report claims that Zheng He returned to Ceylon to capture the island's most sacred relic, the *dalada*—Buddha's tooth. According to this description, Zheng He was delighted with his trophy, as was his crew, who attributed magical powers to it. "The tooth shone brightly," according to one commentator. "Everyone was amazed and turned their eyes from it. They encountered gigantic waves for hundreds of miles, but these did not disturb the ships for the fleet seemed to move across dry land. The fierce dragons beneath the sea and dangerous fish let the ships pass. The men were happy."

Home Port

The ships docked in Nanjing, and the precious Buddha's tooth arrived in the capital—Beijing—on July 9, 1411, ending the third voyage of the epic Treasure Fleet. Zhu Di took possession of the relic and safeguarded it in a special case fashioned of diamonds and jewels.

The Forbidden City

Zheng He received countless honors and tributes after he arrived home in June 1411. The grand director had effectively conquered a large swath of the known world for China, affirming the emperor's status as the most powerful leader on Earth.

The emperor's court became a hub for international ambassadors, with guests hailing from Calicut, Cochin, Malacca, and even Java. The dignitaries came bearing gifts, and what gifts! Horses, leopards, tigers, and elephants were all accepted and inspected, along with gold, silver, gems, and fabrics the emissaries had brought from their cities. All items of tribute wound up in the Ministry of Revenue.

The visiting envoys were treated to imperial hospitality and were lodged in the Hui Tong Hall in Nanjing,

A scroll depicting the Forbidden City, including its chief architect, dating from the mid-fifteenth century.

where they were cared for by no less than four hundred servants, in addition to the physicians who were on call day and night in case the visitors from afar fell sick.

The emperor treated his guests to feasts the likes of which most had never seen at home; the higher their rank, the more lavish the food and drink served. Ministers of the highest rank sampled five kinds of wine, a variety of fruits, noodles, horsemeat, lamb, pancakes, bread, and flower tea surrounded by fine pastries.

After the feasts, guests availed themselves at the *jiu lou*—bars—to be entertained by the *guan ji*, or courtesans. There were also polo matches, horse races, and archery contests staged for the visiting dignitaries. The archery featured contestants galloping on horseback around a target, trying to hit it from a great distance, accompanied by the trilling of flutes and the pounding of drums. Winners received prizes as scholars orated to the crowds.

Despite these festivities, the VIP guests' lives in Nanjing were carefully regulated. They received wooden passports that they had to carry with them at all times. Whenever they entered or exited their guest house, the passport was stamped. They were not permitted to wander freely around the streets, or to talk with the people they happened to meet. Nor could they purchase things freely. It was a crime for them to buy books.

It would be several decades before the West enjoyed the benefits of printed books, thanks to the commercial availability of the Gutenberg press in 1450. The Chinese had been printing books in large quantities since the ninth century, perhaps even earlier, and they were aghast at the thought that books that might contain sensitive information about battalions might fall into the hands of foreigners who would use this information in a malicious way, so foreigners were forbidden to buy books of any kind.

The same restrictions applied to weapons and tools, and even to medicinal herbs. Anyone who violated these constraints would be shackled for a month and sent into exile.

Still, the foreigners did bring one very important innovation with them, *aidai*, or eyeglasses, worth a small fortune in gold. Unlike so many other technological innovations, eyeglasses are believed to have been developed not in China, but in the West, in Venice, sometime between 1268 and 1289. These early eyeglasses were too heavy to wear—so heavy, in fact, that they could only be held in place by hand. They were made not of glass, but of natural crystal, and the view through them was blurry. It was not long before glassblowers in China, perhaps brought to the country by Zheng He on one of his voyages, started to fashion lighter, more practical versions.

—

Zhu Di was attempting to conquer not only the seas; he also had his eye set on the conquest of land. As Zheng He navigated the oceans, Zhu Di erected a new imperial palace in Beijing and expanded the square footage of his mainland empire to glorify his reign.

In 1406, one year after the Treasure Fleet left Nanjing on its maiden voyage, construction of the Forbidden City began. The city was deemed "forbidden" because the emperor's permission was required for people to enter and exit.

Zhu Di commissioned a Vietnamese eunuch named Juan An to design a compound of 980 buildings covering about 180 acres. Construction was a massive undertaking; according to some accounts, as many as a million personnel worked on the site during the fourteen years of construction.

They dragged logs from the jungles of southwestern China, and marble from quarries located nearer to Beijing. Special golden roof tiles were also fabricated.

These tiles were very hard and polished with tung oil—derived from the seed of the tung tree (*Vernicia fordii*)—to make them glisten and produce a ringing sound when struck.

According to legend, the Forbidden City contained 9,999 rooms, considered the maximum number of chambers the emperor could have on earth. In the heavens, he could have the full complement of 10,000 rooms at his disposal. In reality, there were about a thousand less than that number. Nevertheless, it was a fantastic amount of space.

It was a walled city, or, to be more precise, it contained walls within walls, the outermost one about thirty-three feet high. No building in Beijing could be higher than that during the reign of the Yongle emperor.

There were vast troves of art, including paintings and pottery made of porcelain. In 1925, an audit of the Forbidden City counted more than a million pieces of ceramic ware, statues, jade objects, and paintings stored within its walls.

The imperial family lived in the inner court, called the *nei ting*. It held three palaces: the *Kunning gong* (Palace of Earthly Tranquility), the *Qianqing gong* (Palace of Heavenly Purity), and the *Jiaotai dian* (the Hall of Union). Other palaces, pavilions, and courtyards contained particular areas reserved for the empress and the concubines.

The imposing facade of the Forbidden City in Beijing, which served as the imperial palace beginning in 1420. It was considered "forbidden" because no one could enter without the emperor's permission. It has been a UNESCO World Heritage Site since 1987.

In 1408, shortly before the second voyage of the Treasure Fleet, the emperor sent a eunuch on a secret mission to find women to populate the harem of the Forbidden City. Not just any women would do. They were going to be concubines of the emperor, which meant they had to be the most beautiful and desirable women in the world. For the Yongle emperor, this standard could be met only by Korean virgins. The ruler of Korea, unwilling to displease his more powerful neighbor, complied with the demand, assigning officials to scour the country for the emperor's concubines. Those who tried to resist, such as parents who cut off their daughters' hair to make them less attractive, were arrested and deprived of their possessions.

Among the girls who were enlisted to serve the Yongle emperor was the fourteen-year-old daughter of a bureaucrat. She was called Lady Cui, and she was whisked hundreds of miles from her home to the Forbidden City. She never saw her family again, and she secretly wrote about her privileged, cloistered life in the Yongle emperor's harem.

VOYAGE IV

Outward Bound

With the construction of the Forbidden City well under way and China's identity affirmed as the ruler of the southern seas, Zhu Di gave an edict for the fourth voyage on December 18, 1412. The emperor coveted the island of Hormuz, the Persian Gulf city overflowing with wealth and culture, and he entrusted his favorite eunuch with the difficult task of capturing the island's loyalty. Hormuz was renowned as an ancient center for commerce among the peoples of the Arabian Peninsula, India, and East Africa. It was known for its gold, silver, pearls, gems, cinnabar, iron, salt, and copper. The global significance of Hormuz was eloquently summarized in an Arab proverb: "If all the world were a golden ring, Hormuz would be the jewel."

Zhu Di ordered the most impressive array of ships yet, with sixty-three treasure ships and 27,670 crew members all under the leadership of Zheng He. Such a massive fleet was necessary for two main reasons: to ferry back home the numerous dignitaries who had earlier traveled to the Forbidden City to pay tribute, and to achieve the goal of expanding China's influence into the Persian Gulf.

—

The fleet left Nanjing during the fall of 1413 and idled for the next few months along the Fujian coast to await the monsoon winds. The ships finally departed in January 1414.

Zheng He led his men along the familiar route, calling on the traditional Treasure Fleet destinations now under Chinese hegemony. They crossed the South China Sea to Champa, and after a brief visit they continued to Java. Next came the Malay Peninsula, including a stop at Palembang.

The dignitaries had willingly accepted Chinese suzerainty—a system in which a dominant foreign nation, China in this case, controls the foreign policy of a region abroad while allowing that region independent governance internally.

In Palembang, for example, Zheng He had overthrown the pirate chief, Chen Zuyi, and replaced him with the merchant informant, Shi Jinqing, who accepted Chinese dominance in return for military fortification, political standing, and trade entitlements. Within his territory, however, Shi Jinqing was free to rule as he pleased. Zhu Di's political vision was, in many instances, mutually beneficial.

After peaceful trading and uneventful stops along the Malay Peninsula, a small part of the fleet departed to visit Bangladesh while the rest of the fleet made for Semudera on the north coast of Sumatra.

——

The Chinese called Semudera *Liuqui*, which translates to "sulfur ball." The name reflected the region's environment, which was made naturally yellow by sulfur deposits. Ma Huan described how the "mountains produce sulphur, which comes from the inside of caves; plants and trees will not grow on the mountainside; the earth and rocks are all a bright yellow color." Sulfur was a valuable ingredient in Chinese medicines, and because of this, the area had captured the interest of Emperor Zhu Di.

Beyond obtaining the deposits of sulfur, having good relations with Semudera was critical for future Treasure Fleet voyages and exploration because of its geographical location. Ma Huan described Semudera as the "most important port of assembly for the Western Ocean." What he meant by this bold statement was that Semudera was the prime location for the Treasure Fleet to anchor and ready itself before embarking for the Indian Ocean. Semudera thus became an integral port of call along China's trade route.

Political turmoil in the region complicated the emperor's agenda. To solve this problem, Zhu Di ordered Zheng He to impose peace. Semudera, like it or not, would bend to the will of the Yongle emperor.

The conflict in Semudera had begun in 1407 during a

raid, when its king had been killed with a poison arrow by the "tattooed-face king." The "tattooed-face king" received his descriptive title because of the facial scars of his followers. Ma Huan described how "the subject population all have three pointed blue marks scratched on the face as a symbol."

The king of Semudera left behind a son too young to assume his father's throne. In an attempt to restore order, the queen vowed to wed any man bold enough to "avenge my husband's death and recover his land." A local fisherman, moved by the queen's plea, raised an army and executed the tattooed-face king in battle. True to her pledge, the queen married the fisherman and shared her land with him. The fisherman was crowned and became known by the people of Semudera as *lao wang*, or "the old king."

Years later, when the prince came of age, he coldly murdered his stepfather in order to assume what he felt was his rightful place as the sole ruler of the kingdom. The fisherman king's younger brother, Sekandar, was enraged by his brother's unjust death. In retaliation, he convinced thousands of citizens to follow him into the "jungle-covered mountains" to plan a rebellion.

The prince was in a dangerous predicament; he had usurped the throne and feared Sekandar's militia. In a desperate bid to secure his safety, the prince sent envoys to the Ming court to offer gifts and plead for protection.

Embracing the tributary gesture, Zhu Di took the

side of the prince, promising to safeguard him from Sekandar. After all, if Zhu Di controlled the political situation in Semudera, he could guarantee safe anchorage for his fleet in Sumatra. True to his word, Zhu Di delivered a defender in the form of Zheng He and his massive Treasure Fleet army in 1415.

When the Treasure Fleet approached the coast of Sumatra, it came upon an estuary described by Ma Huan as "a large stream of quite fresh water flowing out into the sea; [and] the tidal water flows and ebbs twice a day. In the estuary, the waves are large and ships are constantly sinking." None of Zheng He's ships sank.

When they reached Semudera, Zheng He presented his usual array of treasures, including silks and porcelain for trade, and he lavished gifts from the emperor himself upon the grateful prince. This display of generosity sent Sekandar into a rage. *Why hadn't China recognized him as the rightful ruler?* Furious, he rallied his army of ten thousand men and marched them from the leafy mountaintop jungles down to the shoreline of Semudera to attack the fleet in the harbor.

It was the beginning of yet another battle. Details about the conflict are sparse, but in all likelihood, thousands of Treasure Fleet troops disembarked from their vessels and proceeded to fight Sekandar's army on land with fiery arrows, poison grenades, swords, and explosive devices. Zheng He fought the prince's war with the full might of the Treasure Fleet behind him, and true to form, he overwhelmed the rebellion and emerged victorious.

Like Chen Zuyi, the notorious pirate from Palembang, Sekandar became a symbol of resistance to Ming hegemony and was taken back to China as a prisoner, along with his family. His fate was determined by Emperor Zhu Di, who ordered his public execution. Thanks to Zheng He's army, the prince now ruled unopposed, and he was eternally grateful for the assistance of China. And so Semudera on the island of Sumatra was now secure for safe anchorage along the trade route of the Treasure Fleet.

With peace restored to the region, Zheng He and the fleet sailed southwest for ten days, to the Maldives islands to gather local goods and offer treasures for trade. According to Ma Huan, the islands were always "hot like summer" and were "surrounded by the sea on all four sides . . . In the middle of the sea there is a stone gate, resembling a gate way in a city wall."

The lifestyle of many of the islanders was primitive compared to Ming Chinese society; the inhabitants, he said, "dwell all in caves, they know nothing about rice and grain, and they only catch fish and shrimps to eat; they do not understand wearing clothes and they use the leaves of trees to cover themselves in front and behind."

Fei Xin recorded a very similar impression, describing inhabitants who nested in trees and rested in caves, living on a diet of fish and shrimp. It was all very unlike life in China.

On one island in the Maldives, the fleet encountered a group of Muslims dressed in white cotton. They sold coconuts and an array of products made from coconuts to foreign merchants from around the world. Among the items they offered for trade were coconut shells that had been transformed into wine cups and coconut fibers that had been woven into ropes.

Ma Huan described the fascinating rope-making process: "the fibre which covers the outside of the coconut is made into ropes, both thick and fine . . . Men come from every place on foreign ships to purchase these too; they sell them in other countries for building ships."

Another valuable local commodity purchased by Zheng He in the Maldives was ambergris, the secretion from sperm whale intestines that was used in Chinese medicine and perfumes.

After completing their stay in the Maldives, the fleet sailed west to India. They lingered briefly in Calicut and Ceylon before pushing farther west than ever before, past the Indian coastline toward their main destination, the city of Hormuz in the Persian Gulf.

After traveling with a steady wind for twenty-five days at a rate of forty-five nautical miles (about fifty-two miles) per day, the massive fleet arrived at the mouth of the Persian Gulf.

Hormuz was set against a mountainous backdrop. Its port was located near modern-day Bandar 'Abbas on the southern coast of Iran. It was originally part of the Kingdom of Ormus, founded by Arab princes in the tenth century. By 1262, the area had fallen under the suzerainty of Persia. Since then, the prince of Hormuz had paid dues to the sultan of Persia.

The port of Hormuz was one of the most vital in the Middle East; its strategic position on the Persian Gulf enabled its ruler to regulate trade between India and East Africa as well as land traffic between Iraq and Persia. Hormuz was one of the greatest emporiums of trade in the world, offering the finest luxury goods.

Ma Huan was obviously impressed by the wealth of the people, painting a picture of an almost utopian society: "Foreign ships from every place and foreign merchants traveling by land all come to this country to attend the market and trade; hence the people of the country are all rich . . . Their clothing and hats are handsome, distinctive and elegant . . . There are no poor families; if a family meets with misfortune resulting in poverty, everyone gives them clothes and food and capital, and relieves their distress."

The king of the country and all his followers were also Muslim, Ma Huan was pleased to report. He described the people of Hormuz as "sincere believers . . . Every day they pray five times," with "customs . . . pure and honest."

The people of Hormuz wrote in classical Arabic and followed traditional Muslim practices regarding marriages and funerals. When a man died, "they use a white foreign cloth to robe [the body] . . . They have a pitcher full of clean water, and take the body and wash it from head to foot two or three times; after the cleansing, they fill the mouth and nose of the body with musk and camphor; then they wrap it in shrouds, put it in a coffin and bury immediately."

Ma Huan also recorded the ebb and flow of natural elements such as the weather and the mountains. He noted that the climate varied between "cold weather and hot weather, in the spring the flowers bloom, and in the autumn the leaves fall; they have frost, no snow; rain is rare, the dew is heavy." The large mountain that bordered the port seemed to produce four different products from each face of the mountain: "One face produces salt . . . red in color . . . One face produces red earth . . . One face produces white earth like lime; it can be used for white washing walls. One face produces yellow earth—like the yellow colour of turmeric."

In terms of cuisine, Ma Huan described pomegranates "as large as teacups" and apples "as big as [one's] fist—very fragrant and delicious." Butter was the fat of choice for cooking, and interestingly, much of the local population purchased precooked food from the marketplace to feed their families.

An array of shops formed a backdrop for skillful street performers and acrobats. One man's goat balanced on top of a pole, while another man performed magic tricks with a three-foot-tall monkey. For the grand finale, the man "directs a bystander to take a kerchief, fold it up several times, and tie it tightly round both eyes of the monkey; he directs a different person to give the monkey a surreptitious hit on the head and hide himself in the thick of the crowd; after this [the man] releases the kerchief and directs [the monkey] to seek out the person who struck him on the head; however vast the crowd, the monkey goes straight to the man who originally [struck him] and picks him out; it is most strange."

Beyond the spectacle, the merchandise offered for trade was simply dazzling. Ma Huan enthusiastically described goods from "every foreign country," including all manner of gems such as sapphires, emeralds, rubies, diamonds, and giant pearls. There were also "jade utensils, crystal utensils, and ten kinds of flowered pieces of brocaded velvet" as well as "all kinds of foreign kerchiefs with blue and red silk embroidery."

Under the direction of Admiral Zheng He, the treasure ships unloaded their massive haul of silk and porcelain to make room for valuable stones, metals, and salt that would soon fill the bulkheads for the remainder of the voyage.

To pay tribute to the Yongle emperor, the king of Hormuz "took a ship and loaded it with lions, a giraffe, horses, pearls, precious stones, and other such things, also a memorial to the throne [engraved on] a golden leaf." The Arabian horses were highly prized for their speed and intelligence. They were distinguished by having one less vertebra than other horse breeds, which enabled them to transport riders at great speeds across difficult desert terrain.

Homeward Bound

Envoys from Hormuz boarded the treasure ships for the return trip to Nanjing. China's sphere of influence had reached a pinnacle, and the quest for treasures for Yongle's new palace had been successful. The time had come for the fleet to sail home.

The fourth voyage ended on August 12, 1415, with a remarkable haul of treasures and visiting dignitaries. Shortly after disembarking, Zheng He presented Sekandar to the emperor, and the prisoner was swiftly executed.

VOYAGE V

November 1416 marked the end of an era for the Yongle emperor. In the span of a few short years, Beijing would become the official imperial capital of the Ming Dynasty, replacing centuries of royal residency in Nanjing. It was only fitting that such a forward-thinking emperor should erect a new imperial palace, the Forbidden City, to honor his revolutionary will.

Thanks to the success of the Treasure Fleet, Zhu Di and Zheng He were the masterminds of a trade route spanning from China to Arabia. Next stop: Africa.

For now, the Yongle emperor was content to receive tributes from loyal foreign countries in a majestic ceremony at court in Nanjing on November 19, 1416.

Ambassadors, envoys, military officers, civil officers, and princes filled the palace court with gifts. Gold, gems, pearls, spices, horses, elephants, rhinoceroses, and other foreign goods were offered to the emperor as tribute. The emperor in turn presented "robes with linings of patterned silk" to the nineteen diplomats.

On December 28, Zhu Di ordered Zheng He to return the visiting dignitaries to their respective countries, igniting preparations for the fifth voyage of the awe-inspiring Treasure Fleet. While the exact number of ships and personnel for this voyage is unknown, the cargo in the hulls of the ships was well documented. The compartments were filled with personal letters from the emperor, thin silk, gauze, and porcelain sent as parting gifts for the visiting envoys.

Separating from the rest of the dignitaries, the king of Cochin departed with a trove of symbolic items cementing Cochin's relationship with China. Five years earlier, Cochin had sent a tributary mission to Yongle's court to request an imperial seal to demonstrate its loyalty to the empire. Like Palembang, which under China's sphere of influence kept Siam and Java in check, Cochin pacified Calicut, ensuring that China remained the dominant player along the trade route.

The king of Cochin had been given his seal and a lengthy inscription written by the emperor himself. In the inscription, Zhu Di expressed his warm sentiments for Cochin and the philosophy of his foreign reign:

The world does not have two ultimate principles and people do not have two hearts...How can they be divided into the near and the distant!...I rule all under heaven and soothe and govern the Chinese...I look on all equally and do not differentiate between one and the other...I wish all of the distant lands and foreign regions to have their proper places.

Formalizing China's rule over Cochin, Emperor Yongle named it State Protecting Mountain.

Outward Bound

In the autumn of 1417, the Treasure Fleet left the Nanjing shipyards and traveled along the Chinese coast to Quanzhou in Fujian province. The ships idled there for many months to take on porcelain, silks, and teas. The fifth Treasure Fleet voyage would soon head into open waters, bound for a new land: Africa.

But first, while in Quanzhou, Zheng He burned incense at local temples in tribute to Tianfei and asked for her divine protection at sea. He also worshipped at the mosque by the harbor and visited the graves of Muslim prophets on the outskirts of the city. Zheng He, a master of spiritual duality, fulfilled both his Muslim duties and his Buddhist obligations to ensure that it would be a safe and successful journey to Africa.

Departing Fujian, the voyage followed the route established by the previous four voyages. The ships sailed at an average speed of about 2.5 knots, taking them sixty-nine miles per day.

When the ships reached Hormuz, they sailed into uncharted waters, and the exhilaration of the unknown thrilled the admiral and his crew.

Giant square mainsails filled with wind as the armada ventured southwest along the Arabian coast toward the Red Sea. They continued on their course, sailing through waters that appeared russet from a certain type of algae (*Trichodesmium erythraeum*), until they reached Aden, a land of riches, massive gemstones, and sultans.

The coastline of the city of Aden, in Yemen, was peppered with stone homes. The locals were Muslim and were described by Ma Huan as "rich . . . and numerous," with an "overbearing disposition."

The country was so wealthy that most of the women bedecked themselves with "gem-stones and pearls." Ma Huan went on: "In the ears they wear four pairs of gold rings inlaid with gems; on the arms they bind armlets and bracelets of gold and jewels; on the toes they also wear toe-rings . . . They cover the top of their head with an embroidered kerchief of silk, which discloses only the face."

The region was protected by "seven or eight thousand well-drilled horsemen and foot-soldiers," the fleet chronicler continued. "Therefore, the country is very powerful, and neighboring states fear it."

Aden had an energetic marketplace with a myriad of shops selling "cooked foods, silk, silk fabrics, books and every kind of article." Ma Huan declared the gold and silver produced in Aden to be "the most refined and ingenious . . . which certainly surpass anything in the world."

When the sultan al-Malik an-Nasir Salah-ad-Din Ahmad heard about Zheng He's arrival, he cordially welcomed him at the shoreline. The sultan was dressed in a gold hat, "a yellow robe," and a golden "belt adorned with jewels." To display the riches of his land, he inundated the admiral with precious gifts as tributes for Emperor Yongle and treated the Chinese to a ceremony of welcome "with great reverence and humility."

Sultan Ahmad had ruled the port city of Aden since 1400. He was the eighth ruler of the Rasulid Dynasty, which had wrestled Yemen away from Egypt. This land grab caused a great deal of tension in the region, especially because Ahmad planned to expand his territory even farther southward.

Wanting the backing of the Yongle emperor, Sultan Ahmad had sent four separate tributary missions to China with lavish gifts for the emperor. That was why he so affectionately welcomed Zheng He.

Zheng He traded his usual array of silk, gold, and porcelain for "rare gems, and large pearls, and several stems of coral-trees . . . golden amber, rose-water, lions, golden-spotted leopards, 'camel-fowls' [ostriches], and white pigeons." The Treasure Fleet prepared to depart for its next destination as the sailors contemplated what lay ahead. The time had finally come for Zheng He to lead his men to Africa.

———

Sailing south of Arabia, the fleet glided around the magnificent Horn of Africa—the easternmost part. The air carried the unmistakable scent of land. The ships navigated along the coastline until they reached Mogadishu, in today's Somalia. Here, the fleet encountered miles of settlements with three-story homes made of coral limestone and gardens bursting with citrus trees. The locals were Muslim and spoke a language unknown to the fleet: Swahili. They were extremely mistrustful of the foreign visitors. One can only imagine the shock and terror the towering ships of the Treasure Fleet, with their fiery red sails, must have inspired along the coast of Africa.

Fei Xin found Mogadishu "intolerably hot," and so did the other Chinese visitors. They had descended into a vast arid desert landscape with "nothing but sand." Sandwiched between yellow mountains and sky-blue seas, Mogadishu did not produce much in the way of crops. Droughts were frequent and went on for years at a time. Multistory homes rose from stone piles. The residents were mostly wealthy merchants who traded with foreign ships or simple fishermen. Ma Huan described how both men and women dressed in cotton with ornament-studded cords hanging from their ears.

Here, Zheng He traded his haul of goods for frankincense, ambergris, and "golden-spotted" leopards. As a tribute to the emperor, the fleet was also given lions and zebras. And to Zheng He's delight, envoys from Mogadishu joined the fleet for the remainder of the voyage.

After a brief respite, the fleet sailed on a southerly course along the coast of Africa to the neighboring territory of Brava. Like Mogadishu, Brava sat between the sea and mountains and was built upon parched, lifeless sand. Since there were no locally produced crops, the people survived on a diet of mostly fish. Even the livestock subsisted on fish meal.

In the dry desert landscape, Zheng He welcomed yet more diplomats aboard the treasure ships. When all the crew members had boarded the ships and raised the anchors, they continued south along the Somali coast.

Upon reaching his final destination, Zheng He had the ships dock in Malindi, on the coast of Kenya. From the moment his feet met the shoreline, he was showered with tributes to take to the emperor, including colossal rhinoceroses and elephants.

By this time, the Treasure Fleet had become a veritable ark, brimming with the animals of Arabia and Africa. Zheng He knew his arrival at Nanjing would be full of splendor and ceremony as he pondered the procession of gems and creatures to be presented to the emperor.

HOME PORT

The Treasure Fleet finally arrived home in Nanjing on July 15, 1419, completing its fifth voyage. The ships were bursting with new ambassadors, treasures from distant lands, and rare animal tributes.

Zheng He and his fellow officers were handsomely rewarded by Emperor Yongle for their heroic journey to Africa. And to thank the ambassadors who traveled to China with the fleet, Emperor Yongle arranged a celebration at his court that would live on in legend as one of the most remarkable displays of the Ming Dynasty: an animal parade.

～

On August 8, 1419, the Yongle emperor invited all foreign ambassadors of the fifth Treasure Fleet voyage to come to his court and present their tributes. The envoys would have the opportunity to offer gifts to the son of heaven and, in return, would be blessed with the support of China. One can only imagine the spectacle that was about to unfold.

Drums, bells, and cymbals reverberated off the magnificent open expanse of the outer court of Nanjing. Thousands of singers chanted songs of praise for the son of heaven, setting a tone of widespread reverence for and worship of Zhu Di.

Seated on his elevated throne under the imperial pagoda, the emperor might have been swathed in his finest silk, with large rare gems and opalescent stones from Hormuz and Aden adorning his neck, arms, and fingers. Nestled next to the emperor's pagoda sat the most important court officials, who awaited the arrival of the foreign tributes with bated breath. Zheng He, wearing red, was most likely among the emperor's retinue, along with several other high-ranking eunuch officials.

Up the seemingly endless steps leading to the courtyard palace came a parade of the most incredible gifts ever seen in China. They were all living, breathing, walking—a procession of imported animals. As the creatures drew nearer and the pounding of their hooves and paws grew louder, the excitement in the pagoda intensified.

Leading the parade was a grunting, snorting giant gray rhinoceros with a magnificent horn. Its colossal frame was restrained by ambassadors gripping long leashes. Next came the golden-spotted leopards, whose muscular bodies were tightly held back by harnesses and leather belts. Their bloodthirsty glances terrified the audience around them. The court officials "craning their necks looked on with pleasure . . . stamping their feet when they were scared and startled, thinking that these were things that were rarely heard of in the world and that China had never seen their likeness."

Standing tall, yellow camels with magnificent humps followed in line, as did zebras with their mesmerizing black-and-white stripes. Ostriches pulling hard on their leashes delicately pranced across the court with their long, skinny limbs. Giant elephants and their rough gray hides came next, flashing their gleaming ivory tusks.

They were followed by mighty lions. Ma Huan described how a lion's body resembled "a tiger's in shape; it is a dark-yellow color, without stripes; it has a large head and a broad mouth; the tail tapers to a point, which has a lot of hair, black and long, like a tassel; [and] the noise of its roar is like thunder. All the beasts see it, fall down, and dare not rise; it is indeed the king among the beasts."

Creaky wooden cages filled with pigeons with bright white feathers were also displayed, as were several oryx (a kind of antelope with long, straight horns) and bobcats. To the amazement of the crowd, there emerged the most glorious spectacle of them all. A majestic creature towering fifteen feet in the air caused quite a stir. The creature's head soared high above all the other animals' as it pranced cautiously along the grassy grounds of the court. The beast had fleshy horns, umber spots, an extended neck, and a long black tongue. It was almost silent, except for an occasional snuffling sound.

It was a giraffe.

To Zhu D's court officials, the giraffe, or fabled *qilin*, was a mythical creature. In China the *qilin* held special significance, equaled only by the dragon, tortoise, and phoenix. The giraffe is the tallest animal on the planet, with some reaching nineteen feet in height and weighing nearly three thousand pounds. Their elongated necks fascinated everyone who saw them. Despite its size, the *qilin* consumed nothing but plants and harmed no other living beings.

According to Confucian tradition, the *qilin* appeared only when a sage emperor achieved great goals for his people, so the arrival of a *qilin* at Yongle's court appeared to confirm his legitimacy as the son of heaven, the rightful ruler of China, and the leader of a massive global trade route.

When Ming officials pressed the emperor to accept their official notice of congratulations on the arrival of the *qilin*, the emperor humbly denied his followers. Zhu Di wanted the effectiveness of his government to be recognized with or without a giraffe. "If the world is at peace, even without *qilin*, there is nothing that hinders good government. Let the congratulations be omitted."

In spite of the emperor's modesty, when court officials looked upon the *qilin*, their "joy knew no end." The *qilin* inspired paintings, songs, and poems, including these stanzas:

In the corners of the western seas, in the stagnant waters of a great morass,
Truly was produced a *qilin*, whose shape was as high as fifteen feet,
With the body of a deer and the tail of an ox, and a fleshy boneless horn,
With luminous spots like a red cloud or purple mist.
Its hoofs do not tread on [living] beings and in its wanderings it carefully selects its ground.

It walks in stately fashion and in its every motion it observes
   a rhythm.
Its harmonious voice sounds like a bell or musical tube.
Gentle is this animal, that in all antiquity has been seen but once.
The manifestation of its divine spirit rises up to heaven's abode.

The animal procession marked the apex of the saga of the Treasure Fleet. The Yongle emperor now ruled unopposed over the Four Seas, and his mainland empire was larger than ever before. But despite his unmitigated success, the emperor was struggling to maintain his personal composure as he seethed over rumors of unfaithful concubines.

A giraffe, or *qilin*, of the type sent to the Yongle court from Malindi on the east coast of Africa, painted by Shen Du in the fifteenth century. The tallest mammals on the planet, giraffes were considered to be mythological beasts.

VOYAGE VI

On New Year's Day in 1421, the Yongle emperor formally moved the capital from Nanjing to the Forbidden City in Beijing. This should have been a jubilant moment of celebration in the emperor's life, as he installed himself in the largest palace the world had ever seen.

Foreign ambassadors who had made the long journey to commemorate the occasion celebrated outside the city walls, and within. The concubines were in their lavish quarters, with all their material needs being met. The Department of Entertainment supervised festivals for the women, the Department of the Bathhouse provided them with copious amounts of steaming water for bathing, and the Department of Toilet Paper attended to its particular task.

However, the concubines could not leave their comfortable quarters. Eunuch spies made sure of that. They were everywhere, even concealed behind walls and other barriers, intently listening to the gossip among the women.

It was in this atmosphere of secrecy and suspicion that a devastating rumor spread: The emperor was impotent. Even worse, a eunuch was caught having intimate relations in the spring of 1421 with not one but two concubines, both of whom committed suicide. Wildly agitated, the emperor decided to silence thousands of his concubines for good.

What followed was an event so deplorable that it was expunged from the official records of the Yongle emperor's reign. However, the youthful concubine named Lady Cui, who had happened to be away recuperating from an illness during the purge and thus escaped the terror, wrote about it in her diary. Her scathing account was found many years later.

She revealed that the emperor had wanted to silence everyone involved in this affair. Falsely claiming that his favorite concubine had been poisoned, he ordered almost all of the concubines, 2,800 innocent women in total, to be condemned to death by slicing.

Lady Cui wrote that their bodies were "rent, split, ripped, and torn to shreds," along with those of some of their servant girls and even the eunuchs charged with guarding them. The youngest victims were as young as twelve years old. Some of them cursed the emperor as they died, and others shouted, "We are innocent!"

The bodies were rapidly disposed of, and the emperor thought his awful secret was safe. But Lady Cui's diary recounted, "There was such deep sorrow in the palace that thunder shook all three great halls." She went on, "Lightning struck then, and after all those years of toil, they all burned to the ground."

In fact, a devastating storm struck the Forbidden City the very next day. Lightning destroyed all three of the emperor's palaces. Flames devoured the soaring columns and silk hangings. They even consumed the emperor's throne. The fires were so bright that they cast an ominous flickering light across the Forbidden City. A visiting Persian ambassador said the fire grew so large and intense that it resembled "a hundred thousand torches." The inferno incinerated offices, the concubines' living quarters, and the treasury, and it burned well into the next day. By that time, the conflagration had also taken many lives.

What clearer sign of heaven's displeasure over the emperor's cruelty could there have been? The reign of the Yongle emperor, once so grand and glorious, had reached its lowest point.

"Heaven is angry with me, and therefore has burnt my palace," he lamented. He issued an extraordinary edict in which he confessed to his own sense of fragility:

My heart is full of trepidation. I do not know how to handle it. It seems there has been some laxness in the rituals of honoring Heaven and serving the spirits. Perhaps there has been some transgression of the ancestral law, or some perversion of government affairs. Perhaps mean men hold ranks while good men flee and hide themselves, and the good and evil are not distinguished. Perhaps punishments and jailing have been excessive and unjustly applied to the innocent.

To find the reasons for his rapid downfall, Zhu Di looked everywhere—except to himself.

He tried to make amends by cutting back on government expenditures and lowering taxes. But the moves came too late.

Famine spread throughout Hunan and disease encompassed Fujian, and altogether 253,000 people perished. To survive, many subsisted on wild plants. There was no one left to bury the dead in the countryside. Rebellions broke out and fighting took place, adding to the grief and confusion.

Meanwhile, the embers of the destroyed buildings in the Forbidden City lay smoldering, and it would be decades before the structures were rebuilt.

This sequence of tragedies sent Zhu Di into a steep decline. In an attempt to restore his prestige in the eyes of the people, he turned again to the Treasure Fleet, one of his great successes, and in 1421 gave the orders for a sixth voyage. In preparation for this initiative, he decided to send the visiting ambassadors home with gifts of paper money, coins, robes, and cloth. They had remained in China for almost two years, but now the imperial hospitality was over.

The emperor revealed his new plan to Zheng He. The admiral would ferry the diplomats home and lead the fleet to Africa to explore.

But the voyage was nearly canceled. After all the emperor's excesses, the building of the Forbidden City, and the never-ending military operation in Vietnam, the treasury was running low. Despite the riches the Treasure Fleet's voyages had brought to China, it made little financial sense to dispatch the fleet on another voyage.

Instead, Zhu Di turned his attention to battling dissenting Mongol factions that in recent years had turned against him, refused to pay tribute, and supported his enemies. The finance and justice ministers who opposed this idea were imprisoned, their careers in tatters. The minister of war committed suicide in protest of such a costly military operation in Mongolia.

～

As the Mongolian conflict raged on, the sixth voyage of the Treasure Fleet nevertheless departed, either in 1421 or, according to some accounts, early the following year. Even though funds were scarce, it still included more than one hundred vessels. And in all likelihood, many of the ships also had been part of the original fleet. The one constant was Zheng He, now a veteran navigator and leader who had survived hazards both at home and abroad.

The fleet called at ports of the kingdoms of Lambri and Aru and at the port of Semudera in Sumatra, and split up into several squadrons. One contingent, led by a eunuch named Zhou Man, proceeded to Aden and then about 1,200 nautical miles south to Mogadishu. Meanwhile, Zheng He and a smaller faction of the fleet headed east toward Siam and later north to China, returning to its home port on September 3, 1422.

The official Taizong Shilu, or Imperial Annals, recorded, "The palace official Zheng He and the others, who had been sent as envoys to the foreign nations, returned. Siam, Semudera, Aden, and other countries all sent envoys accompanying Zheng He with tributes in local products."

Three weeks after the fleet returned, Yongle reappeared in Beijing after failing in the third Mongolian campaign he had led. Despite his humiliating defeat, he planned to mount a fourth campaign, and when his ministers recommended against it, he imprisoned them or forced them to resign in disgrace. A month later, he dispatched his eunuchs to secure new sources of wealth to finance another military operation.

～

Despite Emperor Zhu Di's fixation on Mongolia, he commissioned one last Treasure Fleet voyage—the seventh. The date was February 27, 1424.

At the same time, the emperor, who had occupied the imperial throne for twenty-two years, also commenced his fifth Mongolian campaign, from which he

The funerary complex of the Yongle emperor and his wife, the Empress Xu Shi, early fifteenth century, Beijing.

never returned. In poor health, he fell ill and died on August 12, 1424. He was sixty-four years old.

Zhu Di's funeral took place in the gently rolling hills beyond Nanjing. Ten thousand mourners spent two days walking to the site. They traveled in a zigzag pattern to avoid the evil forces that they believed moved only in straight lines.

On the day of the funeral, Lady Cui and fifteen other concubines who had survived the massacre were hanged with white silk nooses in a hall within the confines of the Forbidden City. The sixteen concubines were buried along with the Yongle emperor in a subterranean compound consisting of four rooms concealed eighty feet beneath the earth. They were accompanied by boiled animals offered as food to the gods who presided over ancestors.

The emperor himself reposed in an ornate coffin. Just above his sanctum there was a specially constructed subterranean hall, altar, and courtyards, where rituals would be performed at regular intervals in honor of the deceased ruler. Standing guard over all was an everlasting kingdom in stone: granite representations of warriors, animals, and spirits that extended for a mile, accented by statues of the emperor's ministers waiting in perpetual readiness for Yongle's next command.

Zhu Di's long reign changed China forever, bringing with it dramatic advances—the Treasure Fleet, the Forbidden City—as well as brutal excesses, such as his network of spies and the murders of his 2,800 concubines. Still, he was known as an advocate of ethnic and religious tolerance, including of Buddhists and Muslims. Only the Mongols incurred his lifelong wrath. But still, the memory of his cruelty lingered after his death, as did the fruits of his support for the Ming Chinese culture and empire.

The Yongle emperor was succeeded by his son Zhu Gaochi, the Hongxi ("vastly bright") emperor, who immediately liberalized his father's practices and moved the capital back to Nanjing, as if to erase the memory of his predecessor's excesses.

That shift meant rejecting the decadence of his father and heeding the advice of his Confucian advisers. With the treasury exhausted, he turned for advice to his father's finance minister, Xia Yuanji, a fiscal conservative who had shouldered the blame for the fire that had leveled the Forbidden City.

Not surprisingly, Xia Yuanji counseled that the new

emperor should adopt a program of austerity. The people were suffering and starving at home, on Chinese soil. This was no time to go voyaging and trading in distant lands. "Relieving people's poverty ought to be handled as though one were rescuing them from fire or saving them from drowning," he told a minister. "One cannot hesitate." This austerity naturally meant the end of support for the Treasure Fleet, now regarded as an unnecessary extravagance.

On the very day he ascended to the throne, the new emperor declared: "All voyages of the treasure ships are to be stopped. All ships . . . are ordered back to Nanjing and all goods on the ships are to be turned over to the Department of Internal Affairs and stored . . . All those who had been called to go on future voyages are ordered back to their houses." In addition, he decreed that the ships would no longer be maintained or repaired. It seemed as if the Treasure Fleet had sailed for the last time.

Eight months later, on May 29, 1425, the emperor died, most likely of a heart attack. He was only forty-six. If he had lived longer, the Treasure Fleet might never have sailed again.

———

He was succeeded by his twenty-six-year-old son, Zhu Zhanji, known as the Xuande, or "proclamation of virtue," emperor, who was a moderating force between his grandfather's policies and those of his father. He, too, was a Confucian, believing in the traditional virtues of restraint and avoidance of ruinous foreign wars. He could be exceedingly self-controlled when circumstances demanded it.

For instance, when his hot-headed uncle Zhu Gaoxi attempted to usurp him—much as Zhu Di had usurped his own way to the throne—the young emperor treated the upstart with lenience and confined him to the Forbidden City rather than executing him, as everyone had expected. Zhu Gaoxi took advantage of Zhu Zhanji's clemency by attempting to throw him off balance when the two passed one another, and for this act he paid a terrible price. Zhu Zhanji could no longer restrain his rage and ordered his defiant uncle to be confined inside a copper vat, which was heated until it liquefied around him.

Zhu Zhanji turned his attention to the deterioration of Ming Chinese trade and the troubling loss of the global influence that the Treasure Fleet had built up over the course of six bold voyages. By now the conservative minister of finance, Xia Yuanji, was gone, and the way was clear for the seventh voyage of the Treasure Fleet.

On June 29, 1430, the young emperor declared that Zheng He and Wang Jinghong would jointly lead the seventh voyage of the Treasure Fleet. Wang was a eunuch director who had commanded his own squadrons on the second and third voyages under the grand director,

Zheng He. With great pomp, the emperor proclaimed, "I send eunuchs Zheng He and Wang Jinghong with this imperial order to instruct these countries to follow the way of heaven with reverence and to watch over people so that all might enjoy the good fortune of lasting peace."

VOYAGE VII

On January 19, 1431, twenty-six years after the first fateful voyage, the seventh grand voyage of the Treasure Fleet departed from Longwan, near the Longjiang Shipyards.

Within days, the ships paused at an island called Xushan—its location unknown today—where the men hunted animals in the style of the Mongols. This meant herding them into a circle and moving in for the kill, presumably with bows and arrows.

By February 2, the ships entered the broad channel of the Yangtze River and soon reached Liujiagang, less than two hundred miles from Nanjing, where the ships planned to winter over and ride out the monsoon season.

By April 8, 1431, the immense fleet arrived in Changle, a city of modest size set amid lush green hills directly to the northwest of what is now Taiwan. The fleet stayed there for the rest of the year to provision the ships before embarking on the grueling months at sea.

Zheng He took advantage of the long layover to commission the famous Changle Inscription. It was a massive stone pillar engraved with an eloquent chronicle of the Treasure Fleet's voyages, emphasizing the generosity and kindness of the explorers and taking stock of the admiral's accomplishments. Perhaps Zheng He realized that this would be the last Treasure Fleet voyage, and perhaps he also wanted to memorialize his accomplishments before they were forgotten or distorted by history.

The emperor, approving of their loyalty and sincerity, has ordered us [Zheng] He and others at the head of several tens of thousands of officers and flag-troops to ascend more than one hundred large ships to go and confer presents on them in order to make manifest the transforming power of the [imperial] virtue and to treat distant people with kindness. From the third year of Yongle [1405] till now we have seven times received the commission [official permission] of ambassadors to countries of the western ocean. The barbarian countries which we have visited are: by way of Zhancheng [Champa (Vietnam)], Zhaowa [Java], Sanfoqi [Palembang, Indonesia] and Xianlo [Siam (Thailand)] crossing straight over to Xilanshan [Ceylon (Sri Lanka)] in South India, Guli [Calicut, India], and Kezhi [Cochin, India], we have gone to the western regions Hulumosi [Hormuz, between Oman and Iran], Adan [Aden], Mugudushu [Mogadishu, Somalia], altogether more than thirty countries large and small. We have traversed more than one hundred thousand li [thirty-one thousand miles] of immense water spaces and have beheld in the ocean huge waves like mountains rising sky-high, and we have set eyes on barbarian regions far away hidden in a blue transparency of light vapors, while our sails loftily unfurled like clouds day and night continued their course rapid like that of a star, traversing those savage waves as if we were treading a public thoroughfare...

The power of the goddess having indeed been manifested in previous times has been abundantly revealed in the present generation... When we arrived in the distant countries we captured alive those of the native kings who were not respectful and exterminated those barbarian robbers who were engaged in piracy, so that consequently the sea route was cleansed and pacified, and the natives put their trust in it. All this is due to the favors of the goddess...

We have respectfully received an Imperial commemorative composition exalting the miraculous favors, which is the highest recompense and praise indeed. However, the miraculous power of the goddess resides wherever one goes. As for the temporary palace on the southern mountain at Changle, I have, at the head of the fleet, frequently resided there awaiting the [favorable] wind to set sail for the ocean.

Zheng He eventually got down to specifics, especially of his proudest boast, ridding the ocean of pirates. That feat was just the start:

I. In the third year of Yongle [1405] commanding the fleet we went to Guli [Calicut, India] and other countries. At that time the pirate Chen Zuyi had gathered his followers in the country of Sanfoqi [Palembang, Indonesia], where he plundered the native merchants...In the fifth year [1407] we returned.

II. In the fifth year of Yongle [1407] commanding the fleet we went to Zhaowa [Java], Guli [Calicut], Kezhi [Cochin, India], and Xianle [Siam (Thailand)]. The kings of these countries all sent as tribute precious objects, precious birds, and rare animals. In the seventh year [1409] we returned.

III. In the seventh year of Yongle [1409] commanding the fleet we went to the countries [visited] before and took our route by the country of Xilanshan [Ceylon (Sri Lanka)]. Its king Yaliekunaier [Alagakkonara] was guilty of a gross lack of respect and plotted against the fleet...That king was captured alive. In the ninth year [1411] on our return the king was presented [to the throne as a prisoner]; subsequently he received the imperial favor of returning to his own country.

IV. In the eleventh year of Yongle [1413] commanding the fleet we went to Hulumosi [Hormuz] and other countries. In the country of Sumendala [Semudera, Indonesia] there was a false king...who was marauding and invading his country...We captured the false king alive. In the thirteenth year [1415] on our return he was presented [to the emperor as a prisoner]...

V. In the fifteenth year of Yongle [1417]... we visited the western regions. The country of Hulumosi [Hormuz] presented lions, leopards with gold spots, and large western horses. The country of Adan [Aden] presented qilin [giraffe]... as well as the long-horned animal maha [oryx]. The country of Mugudushu [Mogadishu] presented zebras [huafulu] as well as lions. The country of Bulawa [Brava, near Kenya] presented camels which run one thousand li as well as camel-birds [ostriches].

VI. In the nineteenth year of Yongle [1421] commanding the fleet we conducted the ambassadors from Hulumosi [Hormuz] and the other countries who had been in attendance at the capital for a long time back to their countries. The kings of all these countries prepared even more tribute than previously.

VII. In the sixth year of Xuande [1431] once more commanding the fleet we have left for the barbarian countries in order to read to them [an imperial edict] and to confer presents.

And now, the Changle Inscription proclaimed:

We have anchored in this port awaiting a north wind to take the sea, and recalling how previously we have on several occasions received the benefits of the protection of the divine intelligence, we have thus recorded an inscription in stone.

Finally, on January 12, 1432, the fleet departed. It was a stirring sight: three hundred ships under sail, manned by 27,500 men. The largest wooden sailing vessels ever built bore names befitting their peaceful intent, such as *Pure Harmony*, *Lasting Tranquility*, and *Kind Repose*.

On this occasion, Zheng He's mission was to inform the "distant lands beyond the seas" of the new emperor's reign. It was also, in part, an attempt to restore peace between Siam and Malacca, both trading partners of China. Admiral Zheng He remained a loyal servant to the throne, and he was committed to serving the emperor's will, just as he had served the will of Zhu Di on previous voyages.

The fleet traveled from China to Quy Nhon, the first stop familiar to all the voyages, in southern Vietnam. They arrived on January 27, 1432, after traveling a distance of about a thousand miles. On February 12, the fleet departed Vietnam for Java, arriving on March 7. Here, the giant fleet tarried until July 13, when the ships weighed anchor and made for Palembang, on the island of Sumatra, arriving only ten days later.

On August 3, it was on to Malacca, where Zheng He had triumphed over Chen Zuyi and his pirates. If there were any pirates still lurking in the strait, they did not dare to threaten these mammoth visitors as the fleet sailed into Semudera, on Sumatra's northern tip, on September 12.

There was considerable strategic significance to the fleet's appearance in Semudera, which Ma Huan called "the most important place of assembly [for ships going to] the Western Ocean," as the Indian Ocean was called. On November 2, the fleet departed Semudera, bound for Ceylon's west coast. The fleet was far from land for most of the twenty-six-day voyage, risking unpredictable cyclones and relying mainly on dead reckoning—calculating the fleet's position using a previously determined position and an estimate of their speed.

This passage was one of the few times when Zheng He felt menaced by the elements. The fleet traveled an average of forty-two miles per day—hardly rapid progress. Yet the distances covered and the towering waves unnerved even this supreme navigator. On November 14, Fei Xin noted, "Because the wind and waves were not cooperating, [the fleet] arrived at Great Nicobar Island"—in the blue vastness north of Sumatra and south of the Andaman Islands—"and was tied up at anchor for three days and nights. The inhabitants of the island came out in dugout canoes to trade coconuts and fruits . . . There were both men and women in the canoes."

By this time, Zheng He's health was failing. He was in one of the most remote locations in the world, far from Nanjing—or from any other city. This mountain of a man, who once had seemed to have all the strength in the world, glimpsed the possibility that he might never see China again, and knew that this seventh voyage would be his last.

The fleet finally arrived in Calicut on December 10, and only four days later departed for Hormuz, arriving on January 17, 1433. According to some records, the fleet split up at Calicut. Zheng He remained there, having ordered his assistants to carry out the rest of his itinerary.

——

Zheng He's lieutenants traded with the Arabs for aloe, myrrh, and benzoin, all thought to have medicinal properties.

Meanwhile, one squadron dispatched a detail of seven representatives from Calicut to Jeddah, a port on the Red Sea close to Mecca, the birthplace of the prophet Muhammad and the spiritual center of Islam. To Zheng He and his many Muslim assistants and crew members, Mecca was a destination of the utmost significance. However, it is unlikely that Zheng He himself made the journey. His father and grandfather had both visited Mecca, and it had been his lifelong aspiration to travel in their footsteps. But tragically, he was too sick to undertake the journey, and so he remained behind.

"The land is mostly wild desert," Fei Xin, the chronicler, wrote of the area. "The natural conditions are mild and harmonious, all four seasons being like spring. The inhabitants make a living in peaceful contentment and the customs are such that they esteem goodness. They have a principal chief. There are no obligations or taxes that might cause trouble to the people. Their administration is not based on criminal laws, for they are naturally inclined to do what is honest. They do not produce thieves and robbers, and the upper and lower classes live together in harmony."

Fei Xin went on to record, "In olden times they built a mosque." He was referring to the Great Mosque of Mecca, built in the seventh century. "On the first day of the month, their ruler and the coming people all worship heaven, and this is for the sake of the whole country. There are no ceremonies other than this one. The mosque is divided into four squares, with ninety divisions each, three hundred and sixty altogether, and they all have pillars of white jade, and floors of yellow marble. In the middle, there is a black stone, square [in shape] and more than ten feet in size. And they say it came down from heaven during the early Han period. This mosque has story above story, and it looks like a pagoda."

Fei Xin had a bit more to add about life in this special part of the world. "The men wear long white robes. The land produces golden amber, precious stones, pearls, lions, camels, giraffes, leopards, chi deer, and horses which are eight feet in height; they are the so-called 'celestial horses.' The commodities used in trade with them are such things as gold and silver, rolls of silk, colored thin silk, white porcelain articles with blue decorations, iron tripods and iron pans. During the day, markets are not held, but come together after sunset for so-called 'night markets,' and this is because of the heat during the day."

This glimpse of Mecca, the spiritual heart of the world for Muslims, marked the culmination of the seventh voyage, and yet Zheng He was missing. The unstoppable, heroic admiral who traversed thousands of miles across dangerous oceans tragically could not summon the physical strength to complete the journey of his ancestors. Zheng He would never reach Mecca.

⁓

At some point on the long voyage home, Zheng He died. He was sixty-two years old, and the greatest explorer that China had ever produced. He had opened up China to the world and the world to China.

If he was buried at sea, as seems likely, his body would have been thrust into the water with his head pointed toward Mecca as Muslims in attendance chanted with reverence. At Zheng He's request, his shoes and a lock of his hair were taken to Nanjing and buried at a Buddhist site. There is a grave for Zheng He on the site he specified, but it is rumored among the people who live nearby that nothing is buried there.

The returning Treasure Fleet arrived at the mouth of the Yangtze River in July 1433. By July 27, the officers and other important members of the fleet were in Beijing, where the emperor rewarded them with garments and paper money. Celebrations, including a display of animals such as elephants and the *qilin*, continued sporadically until September, but the emperor, under the influence of his Confucian advisers, cut the festivities short. "I do not care for foreign things. I accept them because they come from far away and show the sincerity of distant peoples, but we should not celebrate this."

Despite the Xuande emperor's misgivings, as many as twelve countries sent ambassadors to pay their respects, until his death only two years later, in 1435.

The end of Zhu Zhanji's reign, combined with the death of Zheng He, brought the era of the Treasure Fleet, unique in Chinese history, to an end. The next emperor

The empty tomb of Zheng He in Nanjing, China. His remains were not placed there because of the great distance between Nanjing and India, where he died in 1433.

ceased construction of treasure ships and embarked upon a course of moderation and self-denial.

The tribute system that Zheng He, with the backing of Zhu Di, had built up over the course of many years declined. No longer did foreign ambassadors arrive to delight the emperor with gifts, and no longer did the emperor bestow his generosity upon his guests. The era of officially sanctioned foreign trade had ended. Smugglers and local markets sprang up to fill the void. Japanese pirates besieged the merchants living along the Chinese coastline. It was no longer safe to traverse waters off the coast of China.

The Treasure Fleet had made its last great voyage, and it had expanded China's trading territory by vast distances. But with the deaths of Zheng He and, earlier, the Yongle emperor, the fleet's glory days were over. The Chinese navy shrank until, by the middle of the fifteenth century, it was less than half of its former size. The decline of China's maritime endeavors was just beginning.

In 1500, it became a capital offense to construct ships with more than two masts. In 1525, an imperial edict ordered the destruction of the entire ocean fleet. Some ships were abandoned, and others burned. The once proud and immense treasure ships smoked, hissed, and crumbled. Any person caught engaging in ocean sailing was arrested. In 1551, it became illegal for any ship with more than one mast to venture into the ocean.

Just a century earlier, China had supported the largest navy the world had ever seen and explored about half the globe. Now the ships were gone, shipbuilders had lost the ability to fashion enormous vessels on a large scale, and the glorious Treasure Fleet itself was in danger of being forgotten.

China had pulled its mighty armada from the sea, and European explorers, hungry for conquest, sailed into the void.

EPILOGUE

Long after the death of Zheng He in 1433, the Portuguese explorer Ferdinand Magellan arrived at a group of islands in a remote location in the Pacific Ocean. It was March 16, 1521.

The existence of these islands, and of the Pacific Ocean itself, had been practically unknown to Europeans when his fleet had left Spain a year and a half earlier. Since he had departed the west coast of South America the previous November, Magellan had expected to reach Indonesia, land of spices, within a matter of days or weeks. Instead, he was still trying to reach the East in search of nutmeg and cloves.

The quest had left him so disheartened that he had thrown his maps overboard in a nautical tantrum and was navigating by instinct, realizing that the globe was much bigger than he—or the best mapmakers in Europe—had imagined. Now, on these distant shores unfamiliar to his native Portugal or Spain or anywhere in Europe, he was sailing into the unknown.

In reality, Magellan had stumbled across a trading post on the island of Limasawa, in the archipelago we now call the Philippines. Chinese merchants had known of this island for centuries. They had gone there to trade porcelain and silk for valuable local products such as pearls, betel nuts, tortoise shells, and coconuts. The appearance of Magellan's armada was therefore not unusual for the islanders, who displayed goods associated with a land known in Europe mostly by reputation—China. Yet there were no Chinese sailors or ships to be seen, only the objects left behind by the Chinese merchant diaspora. One item was a compass more advanced than anything seen in Europe. There were also examples of Chinese calligraphy.

These sophisticated artifacts seemed to have come not from the past or the present, but from the future. What were they? How had they come to be there?

And who had brought them?

BIBLIOGRAPHY

Zheng He is a legendary figure today in China, and he is fast becoming better known in the West. Sources providing information about his life and exploits are occasionally contradictory or incomplete, but a growing body of scholarship about him and about Zhu Di, the Yongle emperor, shines a light on one of the most consequential and exciting periods of Chinese history. We have drawn on the sources described below, in both English and Chinese, to bring this era of rapid growth to life.

Chroniclers of the Treasure Fleet

Fei Xin, *Hsing-ch'a sheng-lan* (The Overall Survey of the Star Raft), 1436, by Fei Hsin. J.V.G. Mills, trans. Roderich Ptak, rev., annot. and ed. Wiesbaden, Germany: Harrassowitz, 1996.

Ma Huan, *Ying-yai sheng-lan* (The Overall Survey of the Ocean's Shores), 1416–1435, first published in 1451. J.V.G. Mills, trans. and ed. Cambridge, UK: Cambridge University Press for the Hakluyt Society, 1970.

Imperial Records

Ming shi ji shi ben mo (Narrative of Events in Ming History from Beginning to End), 1658. Beijing: Zhonghua shiju, 1977.

Ming shi lu (Veritable Records of the Ming Dynasty), 1368–1644.

Books

Anonymous. *Shun feng xiang song* (Fair Winds for Escort) [ca.1430]. *See also* Levathes, Louise.

Bergreen, Laurence. *Over the Edge of the World: Magellan's Terrifying Circumnavigation of the Globe*. New York: Harper Perennial, 2005.

Bergreen, Laurence. *Columbus: The Four Voyages*. New York: Viking, 2011.

Brook, Timothy. *The Troubled Empire: China in the Yuan and Ming Dynasties*. Cambridge, MA: Harvard University Press, 2010.

Chan, Albert. *The Glory and Fall of the Ming Dynasty*. Norman: University of Oklahoma Press, 1982.

Dreyer, Edward L. *Zheng He: China and the Oceans in the Early Ming, 1405–1433*. New York: Longman, 2007.

Hum Sin Hoon. *Zheng He's Art of Collaboration: Understanding the Legendary Chinese Admiral from a Management Perspective*. Singapore: ISEAS, 2012.

Levathes, Louise. *When China Ruled the Seas: The Treasure Fleet of the Dragon Throne, 1405–1433.* Oxford, UK: Oxford University Press, 1996.

Needham, Joseph. *Science and Civilisation in China,* vol. 3. Cambridge, UK: Cambridge University Press, 1959.

Tsai, Shih-shan Henry. *Perpetual Happiness: The Ming Emperor Yongle.* Seattle: University of Washington Press, 2001.

Temple, Robert. *The Genius of China: 3000 Years of Science, Discovery and Invention.* London, UK: Carlton Publishing Group, 2006.

Twitchett, Denis, and Fairbank, John K., eds. The *Cambridge History of China: The Ming Dynasty,* vol. 8, part 2. Cambridge, UK: Cambridge University Press, 1978–1988.

Articles

Church, Sally K. "Two Ming Dynasty Shipyards in Nanjing and Their Infrastructure." *Shipwreck Asia: Thematic Studies in East Asian Maritime Archaeology,* ch. 3. Ed. Jun Kimura. Adelaide, Australia: Maritime Archaeology Program, Flinders University, 2010: 32–49. shipwreckasia .org/wp-content/uploads/FU-South-East-Asia -Archaeology-Brochure.pdf.

Duyvendak, J.J.L. "The True Dates of the Chinese Maritime Expeditions in the Early Fifteenth

Century." *T'oung Pao*, vol. 34, no. 1, 1938: pp. 341–412.

Franklin, Benjamin. "Maritime Observations: In a Letter from Dr. Benjamin Franklin, to Mr. Alphonsus Le Roy, Member of Several Academies, at Paris." *Transactions of the American Philosophical Society*, vol. 2, no. 38, 1786: 294–329.

"Revenge of the Evil Emperor: Mass Slaughter in Beijing's Forbidden City." *Daily Mail*, May 3, 2008. dailymail.co.uk/news/article-563688/Revenge -evil-emperor-Mass-slaughter-Beijings-Forbidden -City.html.

Viviano, Frank. "China's Great Armada." *National Geographic*, vol. 208, no. 1, 2005: 28–53.

Digital Resources

Shipwreck Asia, shipwreckasia.org

The Mariners' Museum and Park, Newport News, VA, marinersmuseum.org

Asia for Educators, Columbia University: The Ming Voyages, afe.easia.columbia.edu/special/china _1000ce_mingvoyages.htm

NOTES ON SOURCES

THE PIRATES OF VOYAGE I

The account of the battle of Zheng He and Chen Zuyi was drawn from eyewitness accounts, primary sources, government records, and scholarly sources.

In "Zheng He's Biography in *Mingshi* 304.2b-4b" from Dreyer's *Zheng He: China and the Oceans in the Early Ming, 1405–1433* (pp. 187–191), the battle is presented in a succinct manner.

Ma Huan, the Treasure Fleet's main chronicler, provides a more detailed and well-rounded record of combat in *Ying-yai sheng-lan* (The Overall Survey of the Ocean's Shores) (p. 10 and elsewhere). He notes that the soldiers of the Treasure Fleet killed over five thousand men, burned seventeen ships, and took the pirate chief, Chen Zuyi, prisoner.

For a more nuanced overview of the battle regarding the weaponry and strategy, see both Dreyer's *Zheng He: China and the Oceans in the Early Ming, 1405–1433* (pp. 55–59) and Levathes's *When China Ruled the Seas* (p. 102). For a comparison of treasure ships to World

War I tankers, visit Columbia University's Asia for Educators site at afe.easia.columbia.edu/special/china_1000ce_ming voyages.htm.

THE ORIGINS OF THE ADMIRAL

The details of Ma He's early childhood and physical development can be found in Dreyer's *Zheng He: China and the Oceans in the Early Ming, 1405–1433* (pp. 11–13, 18-19) and Hum Sin Hoon's *Zheng He's Art of Collaboration* (pp. 6–8).

For Ma He's conversation with General Fu Youde during his abduction, see Levathes's *When China Ruled the Seas* (p. 57) as well as descriptions of his life as a *tong jing* eunuch who was "seven feet tall" (p. 64).

THE EMPEROR

Zhu Di's childhoood education is recounted in Tsai's *Perpetual Happiness: The Ming Emperor Yongle* (pp. 26–28). According to Dreyer, in *Zheng He: China and the Oceans in the Early Ming, 1405–1433* (p. 12), Ma He was Zhu Di's favorite eunuch.

Measurements pertaining to the walls of Nanjing can be found in Levathes's *When China Ruled the Seas* (p. 70). When Emperor Yongle presented his vision of global trade to his dismayed Confucian advisers, he proclaimed, "Now all within the Four Seas are as one family" (p. 88).

CONSTRUCTION

The history of China's maritime prowess and innovative nautical technology, including the magnetic compass, are discussed in detail on the Mariners' Museum website. For more information, visit marinersmuseum.org.

For a detailed conversation regarding the number of ships on the maiden voyage and all other subsequent voyages, see Dreyer's *Zheng He: China and the Oceans in the Early Ming, 1405–1433* (pp. 122–126).

Benjamin Franklin's letter illuminates just how advanced China's nautical technology was. The watertight bulkhead design and adjustable rudders used by the treasure ships would not be employed by European shipmakers for centuries. Franklin's letter can be read in its entirety in "Maritime Observations: In a Letter from Dr. Benjamin Franklin, to Mr. Alphonsus Le Roy, Member of Several Academies, at Paris," *Transactions of the American Philosophical Society*, vol. 2, no. 38, 1786: 294–329.

Zheng He's one fear, "not to be able to succeed," is discussed by Dreyer in *Zheng He: China and the Oceans in the Early Ming, 1405–1433* (p. 197).

VOYAGE I

When Zheng He and his chronicler Fei Xin disembarked in Champa, Fei Xin took note of the king's "three-tiered gold-ornamented cap" in *Hsing-ch'a sheng-lan* (The Overall Survey of the Star Raft) (p. 34).

The Treasure Fleet's other chronicler, Ma Huan, describes local rituals of Java in his book *Ying-yai sheng-lan* (The Overall Survey of the Ocean's Shores) (p. 94), as well as Hindu funeral rituals (p. 95).

Acutely aware of the geographical importance of ports and cities, in the same source Ma Huan refers to Calicut as "the great country of the western ocean" (p. 137).

On the voyage back to Nanjing, Zheng He and his crew encountered an ominous storm and were mystified by St. Elmo's fire, as described by Levathes in *When China Ruled the Sea* (p. 103). The same electrical phenomenon is recounted in the inscriptions at Changle and Liujiagang, according to Dreyer in *Zheng He: China and the Oceans in the Early Ming, 1405–1433* (pp. 145–149).

VOYAGES II & III

When Ma Huan arrived in Vietnam, he was fascinated by the local method of wine making. He outlines the process in *Ying-yai sheng-lan* (The Overall Survey of the Ocean's Shores) (pp. 77–82).

Fei Xin records Java's folklore concerning a devil in the sky in *Hsing-ch'a sheng-lan* (The Overall Survey of the Star Raft) (p. 45). He also describes visiting Pulau Rondo (pp. 60–61) and notes the importance of ambergris (p. 67).

For more information regarding the inscription on the

stele of Malacca, see Levathes's *When China Ruled the Sea* (pp. 107–113). China's generous hospitality toward visiting envoys is also discussed in depth (pp. 118–122).

The complicated saga surrounding Alakeshwara is described in the *Taizong Shilu* (1430), part of the *Ming shi lu* (Veritable Records of the Ming Dynasty), 1368–1644. Dreyer further clarifies the episode in *Zheng He: China and the Oceans in the Early Ming, 1405–1433* (pp. 67–73).

VOYAGE IV

Ma Huan depicts the bustling port of Hormuz in *Ying-yai sheng-lan* (The Overall Survey of the Ocean's Shores) (pp. 165–172) as well as the sulfur-ridden landscape of Semudera and the story of the tattooed-face king (pp. 116–121). Throughout his nautical adventures, Ma Huan also takes note of rope-making techniques.

In Semudera, the crew takes note of the sulfuric landscape. Levathes states the Chinese name for Semudera is *Liuqui*, which means "sulfur ball," in *When China Ruled the Sea* (p. 139). The complicated saga surrounding the would-be ruler of Semudera, Sekandar, is also discussed in depth by Dreyer in *Zheng He: China and the Oceans in the Early Ming, 1405–1433* (pp. 79–81).

VOYAGE V

Dreyer recounts how on December 28, 1416, the emperor bestowed "robes with linings of patterned silk" upon visiting envoys in *Zheng He: China and the Oceans in the Early Ming, 1405–1433* (p. 82).

The reaction of the Ming court officials to the parade of animals comes from Levathes's *When China Ruled the Sea* (p. 151). The political importance of the mythical *qilin*, or giraffe, in China was examined by Dreyer in *Zheng He: China and the Oceans in the Early Ming, 1405–1433* (pp. 158–159, 182).

Ma Huan catalogs the luxury products of Aden in *Ying-yai sheng-lan* (The Overall Survey of the Ocean's Shores) (pp. 154–158). He also describes the physique of a lion (p. 158).

Fei Xin shares his impressions of Mogadishu in *Hsing-ch'a sheng-lan* (The Overall Survey of the Star Raft) (pp. 101–102).

VOYAGE VI

Lady Cui, the concubine who survived the massacre and kept a diary, is discussed in "Revenge of the Evil Emperor."

When 2,800 concubines were tortured and murdered in the Forbidden City, some cried out, "We are innocent!" according to Levathes's *When China Ruled the Sea* (p. 156). Also from that source, after a severe lightning storm set the Forbidden City ablaze, the emperor reflected on his misfortune and proclaimed, "My heart is full of trepidation" (pp. 157–158).

On June 29, 1430, the emperor issued an edict for

the seventh Treasure Fleet voyage, according to Dreyer in *Zheng He: China and the Oceans in the Early Ming, 1405–1433* (p. 144).

VOYAGE VII

For a full transcript of the Changle Inscription, see Dreyer's *Zheng He: China and the Oceans in the Early Ming, 1405–1433* (pp. 145–150 and 195–199).

Ma Huan explains why Semudera was a critical port of assembly in *Ying-yai sheng-lan* (The Overall Survey of the Ocean's Shores) (pp. 115–121).

Fei Xin shares his reflections on Sumatra, the Nicobar Islands, and Mecca in *Hsing-ch'a sheng-lan* (The Overall Survey of the Star Raft) (pp. 62, 104–105).

The Xuende emperor's reserved attitude toward the reinstated tributary system is examined in Dreyer's *Zheng He: China and the Oceans in the Early Ming, 1405–1433* (pp. 162–163).

ACKNOWLEDGMENTS

Laurence Bergreen

Bringing the life and voyages of Zheng He to younger readers has been both an inspiration and a challenge. The accomplishments of this larger-than-life explorer have been celebrated in China but are not nearly so well known in the West. It has been a pleasure to collaborate with Sara Fray, who adapted my earlier book about Ferdinand Magellan, especially because we are father and daughter (or should I say daughter and father?).

Along the journey to publication, we received assistance from a number of dedicated individuals. They include, at William Morris Endeavor, my peerless literary agent, Suzanne Gluck, and her capable assistants, Eve Attermann and Andrea Blatt. I join Sara in saluting Emily Feinberg at Roaring Brook, who proved to be a terrific editor. In addition to the resources cited, I wish to thank Toby Greenberg for providing images and maps and Henry Ferris for his editorial expertise. I also wish to acknowledge the institutions where we conducted research: the Asia Society and the New York

Society Library in New York, and the Harvard-Yenching Library in Cambridge, Massachusetts.

My wife, Jacqueline Philomeno, proved inspirational before, during, and after.

Sara Fray

I would like to thank the libraries at Columbia University, particularly Butler Library and C.V. Starr East Asian Library, as well as Princeton University and the New York Society Library. Thank you to the Metropolitan Museum of Art; the Mariners' Museum in Newport News, Virginia; the USC US-China Institute; the Authors Guild; and PEN America.

I would also like to thank my amazing editor, Emily Feinberg, for her steadfast support and friendship. At Roaring Brook Press, a debt of gratitude is also owed to Elizabeth Lee for her invaluable feedback; Nancy Elgin, Jennifer Healey, and Allyson Floridia for their editorial contributions; Jen Keenan for her artwork; and Mercedes Padró for her design.

To my husband and business partner, Mark Fray, thank you for always pushing me to achieve what I didn't believe was possible. To my beautiful daughter, Zata, thank you for inspiring me every single day. There has never been a prouder mother.

IMAGE CREDITS

INDEX

Maldives, 98–99
Malindi, Kenya, 111
Mandarin writing, 82–83
Mandate of Heaven, 25–26
mang-chi-shih, 52
masts, 35, 36–37
Mazu sea goddess. *See* Tianfei
Mecca, 10, 139–40
medicinal herbs, 29, 43, 80–81, 88
Meizhou, Putian, 68
merchant vessels, 2
Mesopotamian culture, 14
meteorologists, 61
Middle East, 11, 100
Min River, 33, 46, 48
Ming Dynasty, 11–16, 30, 42–44, 105, 112
  combat ships, 5, *30*
  porcelain, 50, *51*
ministers, 12, 87, 123–24, 126–28
Ministry of Revenue, 86
Mogadishu, 110, 124, 135
Mongolia
  conflict with, 8–10, 123–26
  Muslims in, 9–10
  prince Basalawarmi and, 11–12
  service to Ma He, 20–21
  Uighur tribespeople, 8
monkey, 101–2
monsoons, 9, 47, 55–57, 80, 94, 131
mosquitoes, 81
Muhammad, prophet, 11, 138
Musi River, 2
Muslim
  Hormuz and, 100–101
  in Mongolia, 9–10
  Zheng He as, 43, 107
mutiny, 44
Myanmar, 9
myrrh, 138

Nanjing, 9
  attack on, 23–24
  docks of, 34
  festival in, 86–87
  Hui Tong Hall, 86
  Longjiang Shipyard of, 31, 131
  secret passageways of, 25

shipyards of, 28
  voyage II return, 74
navigation, 41–42, 45, 48, 61, 64, 69
nei ting, 90
New Guinea, 29
Nicobar Island, 137
North American, 29
nutmeg, 143

oil, 33, 81, 84, 90
orangutans, 80
Ormus, Kingdom of, 100
oryx, 114
ostriches, 109, 114, 135

Pacific Ocean, 1–2, 8, 29, 75, 143
paintings, 90, 115
Palembang, 4, 94, 98, 106, 132, 134, 136
  harbor of, 2, 53–54, 57–58
parade, 112–16, *117*
Parameswara, 76–77
pearls, 54–55, 57, 93, 102, 108–9, 139
perfume, 15, 99
Persian Gulf, 56, 93–94, 99–100
  ambassador of, 121
Philippines, 144
physician, 43, 87
pirates, 1, 44
  Chen Zuyi, 53–54, 65, 75, 94, 98, 134, 136
  chief of, 4–5
  defeat of, 57–60, 94, 98
  fishermen as, 49
  Japanese, 142
poem, 78–79
poison, 17, 59, 96–97, 120
pomegranates, 101
porcelain, 4, 27–28, 35, 37, 90
  Ming, 50, *51*
  unloading of, 102
  voyage IV and, 97, 102, 106–7
Portugal, *3*, 143
princess of heaven. *See* Tianfei
printed books, 88
Pulau Rondo, 81
putchuck, 81